A Multicultural Education and Resource Guide For Occupational Therapy Educators and Practitioners

by
Shirley A. Wells, MPH, OTR
Program Manager, Minority Affairs
The American Occupational Therapy Association, Inc.

Disclaimers

"This publication is designed to provide accurate and authoritative information in regard to the subject matter covered. It is sold or distributed with the understanding that the publisher is not engaged in rendering legal, accounting, or other professional service. If legal advice or other expert assistance is required, the services of a competent professional person should be sought."

—From the Declaration of Principles jointly adopted by the American Bar Association and a Committees and Associations

It is the objective of The American Occupational Therapy Association to be a forum for free expression and interchange of ideas. The opinions expressed by the contributors to this work are their own and not necessarily those of either the editors or The American Occupational Therapy Association.

ISBN: 1-56900-007-7

Table of Contents

I.

Valuing
Diversity

I. Valuing Diversity

The traditional image of diversity in America has been assimilation: the melting pot, where ethnic and racial differences were standardized into a kind of puree. In reality, many ethnic, racial, and diverse groups have retained their individuality and express it energetically. Many diverse populations are demanding not only an awareness of their differences but also respect for their values, customs, and language.

Culture is an integral part of everyone's life. It is a part of every interaction or personal encounter. In every clinical interaction there are at least three cultures involved: (a) the personal or familial culture of the provider, (b) the culture of the client or patient, and (c) the culture of the medical system. There may also be a fourth culture—the traditional medical culture of the individual (Fitzgerald, 1992). Therefore, appropriate and therapeutic care can only occur if a multiple of cultures are regarded.

This multicultural society requires health care providers to be sensitive to the uniqueness of individuals if they are to respond in ways that are helpful to clients (Clark & Kelly, 1992; Smart & Smart, 1992). It is important for health care professionals to understand and be sensitive to beliefs about health, illness, and treatment. The holistic nature of occupational therapy encourages practicing therapists to respond to all aspects of the client's life— including sociocultural traits that may affect treatment (Jungersen, 1992; Skawski, 1987). The professional mission of occupational therapy—to provide quality service—demands an awareness of and sensitivity to diversity. With the rapidly changing demography and evolving health care system, occupational therapists have been challenged to provide effective health promotion and care to population groups with beliefs, values, attitudes, and behaviors that differ from the mainstream of America.

If cultural differences are not considered, both the patient and the health care professional may find the clinical interaction less than satisfying. Therapists may feel inadequate or incompetent in their treatment. It can lead to the use of an inappropriate treatment model. And it may prevent the therapists from perceiving clearly the needs of the client (Wells, 1991). To respond in ways that are helpful to patients and families, cultural differences must be addressed and multicultural interaction cannot be ignored.

The changing demography of America has also created a work force that consists and will continue to consist of "unassimilated diversity." More than half of the United States work force now includes minorities, immigrants, and women (Thomas, 1990). The survival of any profession will be determined by its ability to be adaptable, to compete more successfully, and to attract all the talent it can find (Morrison, 1992). Therefore, training therapists to manage diversity, to combat discrimination in all forms, and to build intergroup coalitions is a must.

Yet, occupational therapists often lack the knowledge and awareness of cultural influences on human behavior (Blakeney, 1991); therapists may lack the self-awareness and understanding of their own values and attitudes as well as their influence on practice (Wells, 1991); and they may lack the skills and techniques to manage the multiplicity of cultures involved in clinical interaction (Fitzgerald, 1992). Training therapists to be culturally sensitive, to intervene to change biased attitudes, and to become constructive advocates on behalf of other groups is critical. The purpose of sensitizing therapists to cultural factors, stereotypes, prejudices, and ethnocentric judgments in human performance is to improve the quality of occupational therapy practice and services.

Educational programs in multicultural interaction must be integrated across the curriculum. Training in multicultural interaction should include role playing, simulation activities and games, interviews with individuals of diverse backgrounds, critical thinking, and value clarification. Any course or training in multicultural interaction should have both a theoretical and practice component, with clear and specific objectives. Occupational therapy educators must be committed to producing culturally competent practitioners for our profession. Accountability and acceptance must start within the educational sector.

This education and resource guide provides a starting point. Cultural competency guidelines and a proposed teaching module for training and educating occupational therapy students and practitioners in multicultural interaction are covered. Suggested activities, inter-cultural communication tips, vignettes, intervention strategies, and general information about diverse populations are included, as well as an extensive bibliography of articles, journals, videos, and external resources.

II.

Working Definitions

II. Working Definitions

Acculturation: A term used to describe the degree to which people from a particular cultural group display behavior that is like the more pervasive American norms of behavior.

African/Black American: This is a generic term that applies to persons who are Americans of African ancestry. However, in recent years there has been significant immigration of blacks from several Caribbean countries. Because of their shared African roots, many of them—whether native or foreign born—share common beliefs, practices, attitudes, and values. There is much diversity in this population.

Asian American/Pacific Islander: This generic term describes persons whose ethnic heritage is identified with China, Japan, Korea, Southeast Asia, and other Pacific Islands such as Samoa, Guam, and the Philippines. There is great ethnic diversity within the Asian American and Pacific Islander subculture.

Assimilation: The merging of cultural traits; the process of becoming identical or similar to a dominant cultural.

Bias: A tendency or inclination of outlook; a subjective point of view. A strong inclination of the mind. To influence, bend, slant, or lean opinion or feeling, either favorable or unfavorable. To cause prejudice. To this definition may be added: Racist attitudes that discriminate against individuals and/or groups.

Bicultural: Implies the presence and manipulation of two different cultures by one person.

Culture: Refers to the set of values, beliefs, traditions, norms, and customs that determine or define the behavior of a group of people from generation to generation.

Cultural Group: People with common origins, customs, and styles of living.

Cultural Relativity: The idea that any behavior must be judged first in relation to the context of the culture in which it occurs.

People have reasons for their decisions and behaviors, whether or not they can articulate those reasons or an outsider recognizes what they are.

Cultural Values: The standards people use to assess themselves and others. A widely held belief about what is worthwhile, desirable, or important for well being.

Diversity: Denotes an appreciation of, sensitivity to, and integration of differences into an organization and society.

Ethnicity: Highlights cultural as well as physical differences; does not imply that skin color or other physical characteristics have a lesser effect on how people are treated than does cultural background; denotes origin.

Ethnocentrism: The tendency to view one's own cultural group as the center of everything, the standard against which all others are judged.

Gay and Lesbian: These are generic terms that denote an individual whose sexual desires or behavior are directed toward a person of his or her own sex. There is much diversity among this population.

Hispanic: This is a generic term that applies to a group of distinct subcultures. They share many characteristics, values, traditions, and customs, yet there are important differences among and within specific Hispanic groups. Included within this group are people of Mexican ancestry, Cubans, Puerto Ricans, and people from many Central and South American countries.

Individual with a Disabling Condition: An individual with a physical or mental impairment that substantially limits at least one of that person's major life activities; an individual with a record of such impairment; and an individual regarded as having such an impairment.

Latino: Some people of the Hispanic group prefer the term "Latino" because it takes into consideration not only the language, but also the country of origin and shared cultural heritage (see Hispanic).

Multicultural: Denotes the maintenance of several distinct cultural or subcultural forms. "An analogy of this is children engaged in parallel play (several separate and noninteractive activities)" (Kavanagh & Kennedy, 1993, p. 11).

Native American/American Indian: This is a generic term that applies to persons who are native to the continental United States geographic areas (mainland and Alaska).

People of Color: Denotes ethnic individuals; is less offensive than racial minority because it does not imply a lesser status than that of whites.

Prejudice: An unfavorable opinion or feeling formed beforehand or without knowledge, thought, or reason. Any preconceived opinion or feeling, either favorable or unfavorable. Unreasonable feelings, opinions, or attitudes, especially of a hostile nature, directed against a racial, religious, or national group. To this definition may be added: Negative personal behavior that discriminates against individuals of such a group.

Racial Minority: One whose "members are readily identified by distinctive physical characteristics that are perceived as different from those of other members of society, such as skin color, hair type, body structure, shape of head, nose or eyes" (Axelson, 1985, p. 125).

Racism: A belief that human races have distinctive characteristics that determine their respective cultures, usually involving the idea that one's own race is superior and has the right to rule others. A policy of enforcing such asserted right. A system of government and society based upon it. To this definition may be added: Prejudice plus power.

Stereotype: An exaggerated belief, concept, idea, or image about a person or group of people that is held by people and sustained by selective perception and selective forgetting.

Transcultural (Cross-Cultural): Implies a bridging of significant differences in cultural or subcultural communication style, beliefs, or practices. "An analogy of children engaged in playing a game in which effective communication and interaction between or across children occurs" (Kavanagh & Kennedy, 1993, p. 11).

Tolerance: A fair and objective attitude toward those whose opinions, practices, races, religion, nationality, or the like, differ from one's own. A liberal spirit toward the views and action of others. The act or capacity of enduring. Allowable deviation. To this definition may be added: Celebrating diversity.

Diverse Populations

For the purpose of this text, the term *diverse population* includes, but is not limited to, the following:

Ethnic Groups:

  African Americans

  Asian Americans

  Pacific Islanders

  Hispanic/Latino Americans

  Native Americans/American Indians

Individuals with Disabling Conditions

Gays and Lesbians

Religious Groups

III.

Cultural Competency in Occupational Therapy

III. Cultural Competency in Occupational Therapy

Guidelines

Cultural competency is a life long process, ... must continually learn about different cultures and discover the unique cultural background of each client."

—Dillard (1992, p. 725).

The culturally competent therapist in occupational therapy:

- Is aware of and sensitive to his or her own culture,
- Is aware of and willing to explore his or her own biases and values,
- Is respectful of and sensitive to diversity among individuals,
- Is knowledgeable about another's culture, and
- Is skilled in selecting and using culturally sensitive intervention strategies.

Characteristics

Characteristics of a culturally competent therapist include:

- being willing to learn about another's culture;
- acknowledging and valuing cultural diversity;
- having specific and extensive knowledge of the language, values, and customs of a particular culture;
- having a basic knowledge of human development as it relates to race, ethnicity, gender, disabling conditions, religion, sexual orientation, and life-style;
- understanding the influence of culture, gender, race/ethnicity, religion, disabling condition, and sexual orientation on behaviors and needs;
- understanding that socioeconomic and political factors significantly impact the psychosocial, political, and economic development of ethnic and culturally diverse groups;
- understanding the impact of institutional and individual racism on the utilization of the health care system by ethnic and culturally diverse groups;

- understanding the impact of institutional and individual racism on the therapist–client relationship/interaction;

- understanding professional values and codes of conduct as they relate to cultural interaction;

- understanding health-related values, perspectives, and behavioral patterns of diverse populations;

- possessing the ability to decrease the degree of disparity among the cultures in clinical interaction;

- being able to avoid applying a "cookbook approach" to all people associated with a population or diverse group;

- being able to generate, modify, and adapt a variety of intervention strategies to accommodate the particular culture of the client;

- being able to use, send, and interpret a variety of communication—verbal and nonverbal—skills to facilitate the therapist–client interaction;

- being creative and resourceful in identifying and utilizing cultural value systems on the behalf of the client; and

- helping the clients to understand, maintain, or resolve their own sociocultural identification.

IV.

A Teaching Module

IV. Teaching Module

Purpose

Occupational therapists working in the United States today practice in a culturally diverse society. More and more people are choosing to maintain their distinctive cultural identities. With the rapidly changing demography of America and the need to accomplish the mission of occupational therapy—to provide quality care—multicultural interaction must be considered and addressed within the educational program.

Every encounter and every interaction, including clinical, involves a multiple of cultures. "If occupational therapists are to promote maximum competencies in occupational performance, therapists need to know what competent performance is in the context of an individual culture" (Jungersen, 1992, p. 748)

Course Summary

Through a variety of media, lectures, presentations, and activities, the student will begin to acknowledge and understand the impact of ethnicity, race, and culture on occupational therapy theories and treatment processes. Skills needed for the development of cultural competence will be initiated and fostered. Culturally sensitive intervention strategies will also be presented.

AOTA Essentials

OTA: I. c. Knowledge and appreciation of multicultural factors.
II. c. Human behavior in the context of sociocultural systems.
d. Environmental and community effects on the individual.
e. Basic influences contributing to health.

OT: I. c. Knowledge and appreciation of multicultural factors.
II. c. Human behavior in the context of sociocultural systems to include beliefs, ethics, and values.
e. Effects of health and disability on individual, family, and society, including the promotion of health and prevention of disease.
III. b.(2) Analysis of the theories of human adaptation and life satisfaction across the life span, including a multicultural perspective.

Objectives

The student will:

1. Demonstrate a beginning knowledge of his or her own ethnicity, self-identity, values, biases, beliefs, and attitudes.
2. Demonstrate a beginning knowledge of human development and the life cycle as they relate to ethnicity, gender, or disabling condition.
3. Demonstrate a beginning knowledge of institutional and cultural barriers that may influence the therapist–client relationship.
4. Demonstrate a beginning knowledge of institutional and cultural barriers that influence utilization of health care systems.
5. Know the demographic characteristics of each diverse population.
6. Know the cultural characteristics and life experiences of each diverse population that differs from the general white population of the United States.
7. Be able to discuss the commonalities and unique traits as across diverse groups.
8. Know the health trends, beliefs, and practices of each diverse population.
9. Be able to discuss health-related values, perspectives, and behavioral patterns of diverse populations.
10. Know the social relationships and networks of each diverse population.
11. Know the importance of optimal health among each diverse group.
12. Know the role of the therapist as a health care provider to each diverse population.
13. Be able to identify and use alternative roles/methods/points of contact in increasing professional/consumer interaction.
14. Be able to identify cultural issues that should be incorporated into the occupational therapy treatment process.
15. Demonstrate appropriate multicultural communication skills.
16. Demonstrate skills in interacting with individuals from diverse groups.
17. Demonstrate competence in selecting and using culturally sensitive therapeutic techniques.
18. Be able to identify specific treatment approaches that may be effective with each diverse population.

Suggested Content Issues and Topics

I. Definitions

bias	prejudice
racism	tolerance
culture	ethnicity
race	stigma
intercultural communication	stereotype

II. Levels of Understanding Needed to Interact in a Multicultural Environment

A. Knowledge of self

Sensitivity and awareness

self-awareness	attitudes
self-identity	values
perception	

Racism

individual

institutional

B. Knowledge of human development and the life cycle as they relate to:

ethnicity	culture
gender	race
disabling conditions	religion
sexual orientation	

C. Knowledge of professional values

professional code of ethics

III. Information Needed About Each Diverse Population

A. Demographic trends and characteristics

population	income
geography	employment
education	marital status

B. Cultural characteristics and life experiences

cultural themes	history in the U.S.
generational differences	life satisfaction
religion	cultural behaviors
racial factors	heritage and roots
traditions	

C. Health status and beliefs

life expectancy	morality rate
risk factors	morbidity rate
utilization	health practices
traditional practices	

D. Social relationships and networks

support systems: formal and informal

family structures

economic support

utilization of support systems

E. Caregiving issues and concerns

quality of life	death and dying
family responsibilities	support system
children responsibilities	future needs

F. Other issues and concerns

legal issues	living arrangements
housing	retirement
guardianships	
service programs: local, state, federal	

III. Role of the Therapist

health care provider

educator

advocator

IV. Treatment Approaches/Guidelines

Communication skills/styles (verbal and nonverbal)

Interpreters

Avoid "cookbook" approach

Culturally sensitive intervention strategies

Understanding the Impact of Ethnicity on Normal Developmental Tasks

Every man is like all men, in certain respects, like some other men, and like no other."

—*Kluckhohn & Stodtbeck (1961)*

Cultural factors affecting normal developmental tasks

- Environmental conditions
- Historic events
- Economic status
- Child-rearing practices
- Religious orientation
- Political structures
- Male/female roles
- Attitude toward aging
- Time perspective and orientation
- Communication
- Ethnic/racial issues

Levels of Understanding

Knowledge of self-awareness:

- own set of values in relation to the effect it may have on all types of interaction;
- own range of attitudes—prejudices, hostility, fear, suspicion, ingrained racism, own self-identity;
- perceptions of the consumers/clients/patients one works with; and

- sensitivity to one's own ethnicity and the need to value and respect diversity.

Basic understanding of:

- the sociopolitical systems operating in the United States with respect to treatment of minorities;
- the similarities and differences among whites, African Americans, Native Americans, Hispanics, Asian Americans, and other racial/ethnic groups;
- the handicap/disability process and the stigmas that accompany handicaps/disabilities and minority groups; and
- the institutional barriers that prevent or discourage members of minority groups from using them.

Basic knowledge of:

- human development and the life cycle as they relate to ethnicity, gender, sexual orientation, and disabling conditions;
- professional values (behaviors in dealing with all consumers/clients/patients).

Kinds of Racism

A. Individual

Attitudes

Behaviors

Socialization

Self-interest

Interaction

B. Cultural

Music

Religion

Standards, needs, norms

Esthetics

Language

C. Institutional

Education

Economics

Health services

Politics

Housing

Levels of Racism

Conscious level

1. Examples of individual racist attitudes
   a. Belief in white supremacy
   b. Belief that Blacks are genetically inferior
   c. Belief that all Native Americans are savages or alcoholics
2. Examples of individual racist behaviors

a. Bombing of Black churches; lynching of Black people

b. Use of racial epithets ("nigger")

c. Refusal to integrate or bus white children

3. Examples of institutional racist attitudes

    a. Belief in limited intellectual abilities of minorities

    b. Belief in stereotypes shown in media

    c. Belief that affirmative action is reverse racism

4. Examples of institutional racist behaviors

    a. Discrimination against minority home buyers by real estate groups fearful of panic selling

    b. Busing of Black children to white schools

    c. Use of a quota system; tokenism

Unconscious level

1. Examples of individual racist attitudes

    a. Belief in melting-pot theory

    b. Denial of racism

    c. Belief that all people are treated equally in the United States

2. Examples of individual racist behaviors

    a. Laughter at racist jokes

    b. Business dealing with racist companies

    c. Use of anti-minority, biased language

3. Examples of institutional racist attitudes

    a. Assumption that white personnel can meet the needs of all the people in the institution, but that minority staff members can deal only with the needs of other minorities.

    b. Disregard of minorities' needs in developing products.

    c. Disregard of minority cultural perspectives in developing standardized tests.

4. Examples of institutional racist behaviors

    a. Destruction of minority and/or low-income housing in urban renewal to make way for commercial facilities or upper-income housing.

    b. Teaching of (white) American history only.

    c. Consent to the death of 500 or more children each year because of lack of proper clothing, shelter, and medical facilities.

*Culturally Sensitive Intervention Strategies

1. Become aware of the minority group's inclinations on issues of privacy, self-disclosure, familial power and distribution, discussion of intimate matters with persons outside the family, use of formally organized helping institutions, and the context in which help is or should be offered.

2. During the assessment, consider the social-environmental impacts as well as psycho-individual reactions.

3. Become familiar with local medical beliefs and practices. Ethnic health practices are derived from basic needs and fears. Folk medicine, which may be defined as primitive by outsiders, is functional for the persons within the culture. The patient's beliefs must be respected.

4. Take advantage of opportunities to learn about people and their cultures. Listening and showing a willingness to learn and share experiences can be valuable.

5. During discharge/termination planning, make an effort to connect the patients/clients to the positive elements of support in their ethnic community.

6. Avoid recommending and training in use of equipment that maybe financially impractical, culturally inappropriate, or culturally unacceptable to the patient/client and the family.

7. Avoid patronizing or condescending approaches.

8. Understand the communication style of the ethnic group. Observe for any cues, verbal or nonverbal, that may indicate preferences.

9. Develop a wide variety of verbal and nonverbal responses that will facilitate involvement of the patient.

10. Become familiar with special terminology used by the patient/client.

11. Use an interpreter if you are not fluent or effective in a target language. Learn basic words and sentences in the target language.

12. If an interpreter is used, meet with the him or her on a regular basis to discuss information to be given and received from the patient/client, the interpreter's style and approach to the patient/client, and the cultural practices and beliefs. An understanding of the interpreter's verbal and nonverbal style may eliminate some interpreter-related problems, such as changes in message and/or information due to paraphrasing, frank omission, or the combination of two separate and unrelated issues into one. Avoid using family members as interpreters, for they are usually ill-prepared to deal with the complexity of medical terms and information as well as the skills of interpreting.

13. Involve the patient/client and family members in goal setting.

14. Be aware of your personal values and biases and how they may impact the therapeutic relationship.

15. Discuss with the patient/client how potential treatment goals and outcomes may alter typical cultural roles. Let the patient/client decide to engage in new behaviors.

16. Be flexible and adaptable in your approach. Take into account the patient's/client's culture and how it affects and shapes the individual.

17. Remember that cultural values and beliefs are based on needs that may have little basis in environmental realities (e.g., religion is an important factor in shaping the individual's definition of life and appropriate behaviors).

*Source: Wells, S.A. (1991). *Clinical considerations in treating minority women who are disabled.* Occupational Therapy Practice, 2(4), 20–21. Reprinted with permission from Aspen Publishers, Inc.

V.

Intercultural Communication

V. Intercultural Communications

*Self-Assessment Checklist for Communications

Directions: To assess how hard you will have to work to communicate in the multicultural work place, rate your responses in the statements below. Use a scale of 1 to 5 to rate how strongly you agree with the statements; 1 represents low agreement and 5, high agreement.

Rating

_____ 1. I speak slowly, audibly, and distinctly.

_____ 2. I use simple words and avoid jargon or slang.

_____ 3. I listen as much as I speak; I do not interrupt.

_____ 4. I allow extra time to communicate with someone whose first language is not mine.

_____ 5. I respect silence and do not fill every gap in communications.

_____ 6. I consider the effect of cultural difference on messages being transmitted, and I check my assumptions.

_____ 7. When experiencing frustration or sensing conflict in a cross-cultural situation, I ask myself, "What's really going on here?"

_____ 8. I adapt my style to the demands of a situation.

_____ 9. I appreciate different ways of communicating.

_____ 10. I do not judge people based on their accents or language fluency.

_____ 11. I use the telephone judiciously.

_____ 12. I try to be open and direct in giving feedback.

_____ 13. I make an effort to talk about differences. I try to include people in discussions that affect them.

_____ 14. I never make ethnic jokes, and I object when others do.

_____ 15. I never make remakes that are "hot buttons" for women, men, ethnic/racial groups, gays and lesbians, religious groups, or any other group.

_____ **Total**

How to Score:
Total your answers. If your score is:

- *65 or above,* you probably value diversity and are able to communicate with people who are different from yourself—but one always has room for improvement.

- *below 60,* you probably experience much difficulty communicating across cultures and could benefit from further training.

*Source:Used with permission from Resolution Dynamics, Inc., Exploring the Value of Diversity Workshop, (1991) as adapted from Communicating Across Cultures [Valuing Diversity Series, Part 3] Copeland Griggs Productions.

*Barriers to Effective Intercultural Communication

1. **Cultural differences in communication styles, including:**
   Convention for courtesy

   Cultural norms for interacting or differing communication styles can cause misunderstanding.

   Sequence

   Some people line up their thoughts in a straight line leading directly to the point, one step at a time. Others may talk in loops, explore tangents, and elaborate details and variations of the subject along the way.

   Phasing

   Cultural habits also influence people's ideas about when it is appropriate to discuss certain things. For example, in the north, people may value "getting down to business" right away. In the south, more time to develop a "social rapport" before talking about business is the desired norm.

   Objectivity

   To some, logic and accuracy are essential. If words are not precise enough for them, they are driven to ask the speaker to clarify. This may derail others who perceive the relent less precision to be manipulative and domineering.

   In conflict situations, some people prefer to argue impersonally, aiming for objective neutrality, and not allowing emotion to interfere with reason. Others may distrust the motives of people who are emotionless and aloof in their arguments. Conversely, a person who has a more emotive style of arguing may appear too animated and confrontational. The difference in style may replace the content of the issue as the object of the argument.

   Specificity

   People establish trust in relationships in culturally different ways. Some people prefer to get agreement on general principles before committing to details. Other prefer the specifics, feeling that the sum will be the total of the parts.

   Assertiveness

   Some cultures are more verbally expressive than others. Some are very inquisitive and chatty, while Native

Americans, for example, tend to respect silence and privacy.

Candor

To some people truth is paramount; therefore they place high value on "telling it like it is"—no matter how unpleasant the message. Other cultures place a higher value on courtesy and harmony. They are less honest, but have other ways of communicating real meaning. For example, to save face, an Asian employee may say "yes" and it may not mean "yes, as an affirmative" but "yes, I will try. I will do everything to make sure that it is yes." In certain cultures, to say "no" is a blatant insult.

Simplicity

One common mistake people make is to try to impress others by speaking the way they believe more educated people speak. The key to effective communication is simplicity.

Accents

Another mistake is to judge the ability of others based on their accents. People can often react negatively to those with accents or who are stumbling while trying to speak in our language. People also make judgments based on the kind of expressions others use. For example, ethnic minority colloquialisms are often referred to as "jive"; white colloquialisms are "jargon." Whites using slang are often viewed as "colorful," but ethnic minorities using slang are thought to be illiterate.

Telephone usage

In today's fact-paced world, telephone and telex are efficient ways of reaching people. But when communicating electronically with people of other cultures, it is important to use the medium appropriately. Personal meetings may be a more effective way to transact business with others of certain cultures than is a seemingly efficient telephone conference call. It is best to use the telephone to enhance, not replace, personal contact.

2. Assumptions, stereotypes, prejudices, or biased thinking

If the assumptions we make about people go untested, then behavior may reflect stereotypic thinking. Assumptions and biased thinking also interfere with active listening.

Acknowledging our prejudices and managing the impact of them on our decision-making processes are vital to effective communication and interactions.

3. Difficulty talking about differences—(e.g., "walking on eggshells")

Communicating about cultural, gender, sexual orientation, or religious issues. Feedback or performance coaching.

4. Hot buttons include:

Jokes

Words

Swearing

*Source: With permission from Resolution Dynamics, Inc.'s Exploring the Value of Diversity Workshop (1991), as adapted from Communicating Across Cultures [Valuing Diversity Series, Part 3] Copeland Griggs Productions.

*For More Effective Intercultural Communication

1. Learn to listen.

2. Learn to communicate clearly and fairly.

3. Test for understanding.

4. Invite others to be a part of the discussion.

5. Adapt your communication style to the situation.

6. Avoid "hot buttons."

7. Use language that fosters trust and alliance.

8. Don't misjudge people because of accent or grammar.

9. Remember that when conflicts arise, the problem may result from style rather than content.

*Source: With permission from Resolution Dynamics, Inc.'s Exploring the Value of Diversity Workshop (1991).

VI.

Vignettes

VI. Vignettes*

Task: Read the vignettes provided. As a small group, discuss what is happening in the vignette. Use the following questions to help analyze the interaction and how cultural and/or ethnic differences may have played a part.

- What has happened here?
- What assumptions, stereotypes, or misconceptions are evident (explicitly or implicitly)?
- How would you handle the situation?
- What are the implications if this situation is not successfully handled?

Vignette 1: The Joke

You are in a meeting (classroom) waiting for the boss (instructor) to come in. There is a general feeling of camaraderie with many jokes and stories. You realize that an ethnic joke is being told and, as you look up, you see the face of the person whose group has been slandered. You suddenly realize that the person is hurt. There is an awkward silence for a moment, and then general talk takes over and the subject is changed.

Vignette 2: The Patient

Mary, an OTR of African descent, is assigned a new patient. Mary has been a clinician for 3 years and has the reputation of being one of the best therapists in the department.

She visits the patient in the patient's room, explains the purpose of occupational therapy, and starts her initial assessment. Mary feels that everything is going well and is looking forward to seeing the patient the next day.

The following morning, Jean, the supervisor of the department, asks to speak with Mary. "Mary, I know you are a good therapist but—don't take this personally—I am giving the new patient to Sue [a COTA]." "Why?" asks Mary. "I just feel that it is the right thing to do," says Jean.

As the day progresses, there are rumors in the department that the patient requested the change because Mary is Black. Mary decides to confront Jean about what she's heard. "Are the rumors correct?" asks Mary. "Yes, they are," says Jane.

Vignette 3: The Home Visit

Joan, a pediatric therapist, is asked to make a home visit to a Vietnamese child who recently experienced burns. On examination of the child, she notes red, round, coin-sized, marks over the child's back. The mother is never asked about the marks.

Joan reports to the supervisor, "I think the mother is abusing the child and causing the burns herself."

Note: Coin rubbing is an Asian folk practice believed to cure a cold or the flu. Spread a layer of Tiger Balm or Hong Kong oil on the back or shoulder of the patient. Take a coin (a quarter works best), press, and draw it in one direction. If dark blood flushes to the surface, it's a sign that it works. If it doesn't, try another spot.

Vignette 4: The Omission

You are attending a workshop/lecture about a disabling condition and its effect on specific populations. A multitude of groups and populations—Jews, Hispanics, African Americans, Germans—are presented and discussed. The only time that gays and lesbians are mentioned is in connection with the total number of deaths resulting from the condition. When asked by an attendee about the effects of this condition on the gay and lesbian population, the speaker/lecturer ignores the individual and goes on to another question.

Vignette 5: Friends

Five boys are sitting in a restaurant having lunch. They look like a group of typical Anglo-Saxon, middle-class, American teenagers. One, however, is not. He is of mixed heritage, Black and white. His name is John.

Four members of the group have been friends for years and know that John is of mixed heritage. The fifth youth is new to the group and the heritage of the others has not crossed his mind.

As they sit, a couple enters the restaurant. The man could be of Mexican or Indian descent and the woman has blond hair and fair skin.

"God damn! Will you look at that. Nothing pisses me off more," says one of the boys.

The other four boys look up at the fifth, and John asks, "What?"

"See that beautiful white woman hunched all up against a greasy spic. What if they have children? Can you imagine what they would be like, little greasy spics with blond hair and blue eyes."

Vignette 6: Overhearing Indirect Remarks or Comments

You have just overheard one of your coworkers talking on the phone with an OT student. From the tone of the conversation, you surmise that it was not an easy exchange. At the end of the telephone conversation, you hear your coworker saying to another, "I'm sick and tired of dealing with those people; with some of them, you can't understand a word they say. They really dislike taking instructions from women! I'm not even sure you can trust them. Why don't they go back where they came from?"

Vignette 7: The Assumption

Mrs. Jones is in her mid 60s. She is poor and dependent for her existence on food stamps and supplemental security income provided by the federal government. Somewhat hard of hearing, she has a slight tremor in her voice and arthritis in her hands. Her physical environment is incredibly impoverished. The three-room house in which she lives is in poor condition. She has no running water or inside toilet. Near the house is a water pump and an old wooden privy. The house is unkempt; flies and other insects abound. For meals, she relies on her neighbors and junk food.

Mrs. Jones is admitted to the rehabilitation unit after experiencing a mild stroke that leaves her impaired on the right side. Her treatment sessions consist of transferring from the bed to the wheelchair, from the wheelchair to a toilet seat, learning one-handed cooking, and dressing with adaptive equipment. A variety of equipment and devices is recommended and ordered for her.

At the discharge planning session, the therapist states, "Mrs. Jones has refused all of the equipment even though she is able to use them safely and properly."

Vignette 8: Why

Maria has just arrived at her friend Gloria's house in answer to a tearful phone call, in which the latter said she and her boyfriend have broken up.

"What happened?" asks Maria.

"It was his parents. He didn't even have the guts to tell me himself. His mother called and told me that she and her husband did not think that different races and religions mix and that they just thought it better if their son did not go around with a Mexican Catholic."

Maria sighs and says, "Oh no."

"What is it, Maria, this thing about being Mexican and Catholic? Why does it seem to make everything so hard?"

Vignette 9: The Qualification

Steven applies for the director of rehabilitation position at a large hospital. He has more than 10 years of experience as a clinician and a has master's degree in hospital administration. He is presently the administrative director of a small nursing home. The search committee is very impressed with his qualifications and experiences. They feel that he is the top candidate for the job.

The committee is surprised when Steve shows up for the interview in a wheelchair. (Steve has a C6 through C7 quadriplegia.) The interview process proceeds as planned; however, Steve feels the committee's discomfort with his disability.

Steve is called and asked to return for a second interview. "Was a second interview required of the candidates?" he asks. The committee chair says, "No, but the hospital administrator was not here the day of your interview, and he would like to meet with you."

Vignette 10: The Invisible Employee

Sue is a successful OTR who has been the program chairperson for several years. She has a reputation for being hard working and fair. At her regular monthly staff meeting, program issues are discussed and assignments are made. Three of her staff members—Elaine,

Sharon, and Beth—are also OTRs. Jim, the Program Assistant and the only male OTR staff member, has a degree in business administration. Sue gets along well with all of them.

After the latest meeting, Sue was surprised when Jim approached her: "Sue, the first thing in today's meeting I suggested was that we develop an Apprentice Task Force to explore ways to heighten the awareness of opportunities in OT among more of the underrepresented populations in the area. Before I was halfway through, you cut in to let Beth speak. By the end of the meeting, you agreed with my idea, but gave Beth all the credit."

Sue doesn't know what to think. She doesn't remember Beth bringing up the idea in the first place! She wonders, "Is something wrong with Jim today? Why is he reacting in this way?" Sue makes a joke to minimize the situation.

Jim thinks to himself, "Nobody listens to me in this department! Am I of the wrong gender?"

Vignette 11: The Party

At a party you become involved in an argument with a friend, who believes that health professionals should not become personally or emotionally involved with poor patients/clients. "We don't need any more bleeding heart liberals," he chides you. "Beside, they don't appreciate people who try to help them. They don't want to do anything except have a lot of illegitimate babies, live off welfare, and try to force our children to go to school with their illiterate brats."

*Adapted from personal experiences, Experiencing and Counseling Multicultural and Diverse Populations.

VII.

Suggested Activities

VII. Suggested Activities

*Getting in Touch With Your Own Social Identity

Identifying Your Social Roles

1. Circle the items in each of the four sections that best describe you.
2. Place a check mark by the items you circled that seem to be most important or significant for any reason to you at this time in your life.

A:

Lower economic class	Middle economic class	Upper economic class
Militant	Radical	Liberal
Moderate	Conservative	Reactionary
Indifferent	Republican	Democrat
Independent		

B:

Anglo-Saxon America	Anglo	White	Ethnic
African American	Black	Negro	Hispanic
Latin American	Latino	Chicano	Hispano, Latino
Hispano Hablante	Spanish speaking	Asian American	
Pacific Islander American	Oriental	Native American	
Indian American	Amerindian	Other:_____	

C:

Female	Male Married	Single	Separated	Divorced
Wife	Husband	Mother	Father	Step-parent
Godparent	Grandmother	Grandfather	Aunt	Uncle
Niece	Nephew	Cousin	Daughter	Son
Step-child	Grandchild	Sister	Brother	Half-sister
Half-brother	Stepbrother	Stepsister	Gay	Lesbian
Bisexual				

D:	Business person	White-collar worker	Professional	Technician
	Blue-collar worker	Skilled worker	Student	Service
	Provider	Laborer	Other: _____	

How Did You Identify Yourself?

1. I best describe myself as a (an):

Row A: _____

Row B: _____

Row C: _____

Row D: _____

2. According to my check marks, the most important roles in my life at this time are:

_____

_____

Discussion Questions

With the above descriptions in mind, consider the following questions:

1. What are the advantages and disadvantages of being this kind of person in my personal life today? My working life?

2. What are the advantages and disadvantages of being this kind of person in the majority community?

3. What are the advantages and disadvantages of being this kind of person in minority communities?

*Source: Reproduced with permission of the Association for the Care of Children's Health, 7910 Woodmont Ave, Suite 300, Bethesda, MD 20814 from Randall-David (1989) as adapted from Counseling and Development in a Multicultural Society, Axelson (1985).

First Thoughts

Purpose: To identify learned stereotypes and thoughts about people who are different from yourself and how these stereotypes may be a barrier to any interaction.

Directions: Look at each word below and jot down the first two or three adjectives that come to your mind. No censorship of thoughts should occur! Positive or negative, just write and/or say your first thoughts!

Upper Class	African Americans
Gays	Native Americans
Asian	Middle Class
Disabled	Jewish
Children	Men
Irish	Overweight
Elderly	Professional
Hispanic	Mentally Ill
Catholic	Women
Lesbian	White
Poor	Protestant

First Experience

Purpose: To learn how health beliefs and practices and remedies are passed on from generation to generation.

Directions: In a small group, discuss your first experience in treating the following conditions. Include who told you about this remedy. You may include all myths and remedies you have heard or tried.

Hiccups

Minor Burns

Bee Stings

Fevers

Activities for Cognitive Base

Purpose: To provide a broad base of cognitive knowledge about diverse populations.

1. Assume that you have been asked to describe a given diverse population to a class of 5th graders. Prepare a 10-minute presentation you could use to fulfill this request.

2. Assume that you have the opportunity to interview some peeple from a diverse population of interest to you. Develop a set of at least 10 questions that will enable you to obtain factual information from those people you will interview.

3. Select a diverse population of interest to you. Create a multiple choice test using factual questions about this group for your classmates.

4. Identify 10 sources of information (e.g., books, articles, journals, or other media material) about a particular diverse population.

5. Identify a particular diverse population. Then write a paper complete with references, defending the use of a particular OT therapeutic intervention with persons from that diverse population.

6. Develop a list of similarities and differences between two diverse populations.

7. Select any particular point of view, issue, or concern made about a particular diverse population with which you agree. Write a paper, complete with references, arguing the opposite point of view (i.e., you might argue that intelligence tests are not unfair to Mexican and African American children, because these children must function within the majority society).

8. Select a book on a particular diverse group of interest to you. Attempt to recreate the outline the author(s) used to write it. Then identify other pertinent topics that might have been included.

Activities for Attitude Awareness

Purpose: To provide a broad base of attitudes about diverse populations.

1. Identify any particular diverse population and then create a list of at least 10 stereotypes you think people hold about that population.

2. Assume that you are an arbitrator between a group of persons from a particular diverse population and a group from the

white, middle-class, majority. Compose a "treaty" to settle the differences between the two groups.

3. Assume you have the power to enact legislation that would benefit a particular diverse population. List and explain the laws you would enact.

4. Assign each person in a group to be representative of a different diverse population and then conduct a mock United Nations activity by having the representative create a plan for the worldwide enrichment of the human condition.

5. Select any two diverse populations and interview at least five persons from each to discover their attitudes about the other population.

6. Select any diverse population and interview at least five persons from that group to discover their attitudes about the helping/medical professions. Include a question concerning how they feel about being interviewed.

7. Assume that you are the director of a new occupational therapy department in a community with a predominant diverse population. You are responsible for hiring the staff. Compose a list of at least five questions that would give you some indication about the attitudes of the candidates toward this particular diverse population.

Experiential Activities

Purpose: To provide a broad base of experiences with diverse populations.

1. Visit, individually or with others, a restaurant that caters primarily to persons from a particular diverse group.

2. Attend a religious ceremony (e.g., church service) that is intended primarily for members of a particular diverse population.

3. Observe a group of children from a particular diverse population at play. Note consistent behavioral patterns and interaction.

4. Ask at least five persons from each of three different diverse populations about their favorite leisure activities. Compare and contrast their responses.

5. Interview an occupational therapist or other health professional from a particular diverse population. Inquire about the professional problems and issues that he or she most frequently encounters in professional activities and client–professional interaction.

6. Interview health professionals or agency staffs who have worked with a particular diverse population. Inquire about the problems, issues, and cultural conflicts most frequently encountered.

7. Conduct a community assessment for a particular diverse population. Identify all the institutions the targeted population utilizes (i.e., schools, churches, hospitals, and clinics), all the social services agencies that serve the targeted population community, all key community businesses patronized by the targeted population, and the community leaders for the targeted population.

8. Develop a plan to market your services to the community groups and people of a particular diverse population.

Role Playing

Purpose: In the preparation process to work with diverse populations, supervised practice in helping/therapeutic relationships is very important. These activities should help the students/participants put into practice all that they have learned about diverse populations. The following items might serve as initial activities in this regard.

1. Have one person role play the part of an occupational therapist and another the part of a person from a diverse population. Have a third person serve as an observer. Role play an interview session for approximately 5 minutes, then stop and critique the activity. Change roles in the activity and repeat two or more times.

2. Have one person role play the part of an occupational therapist and several other persons role play the parts of family members of a patient from a diverse population. Simulate an initial or discharge family interview session for approximately 20 minutes. Then critique the simulation, offering suggestions to improve the interaction. Repeat the role play, incorporating the suggestions.

3. Prepare a critique, individually or with others, of an audio or video tape of a treatment session between an occupational therapist and a person from a particular diverse population.

4. Solicit volunteers from various diverse populations. Role play the part of an occupational therapist working with them as part of the health care team or as colleagues. Then critique the simulation, offering suggestions on how to improve the interaction.

5. Have one person role play the part of an occupational therapist from a diverse population and another the part of a patient/client from a different diverse population who refuses to be treated by the therapist. Role play the treatment session for approximately 5 minutes; include as many stereotypic behaviors as possible about both diverse populations. Then stop and critique the activity, offering suggestions for improving the situation or relationship. Repeat the role play incorporating the suggestions given.

6. Have one person role play the part of an occupational therapy department manager from a diverse population and several other persons role play the parts of staff members. Role play a department meeting dealing with a controversial issue for approximately 10 minutes. Critique the simulation, offering suggestions to improve the interaction.

VIII.

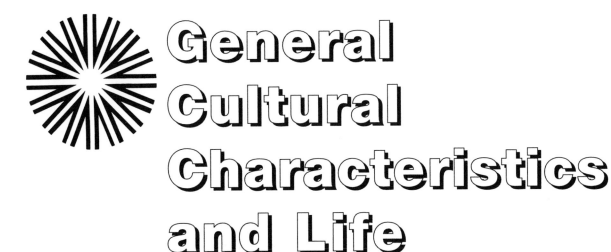

General Cultural Characteristics and Life Experiences

VIII. General Cultural Characteristics and Life Experiences

A person's color [difference] is the first thing we see but, the last thing we talk about...." The following information, descriptions of life styles, value systems, health care beliefs, and communication styles represent only some of the many possible variations that may exist among individuals, families, and groups or cultures. In order to provide quality and effective services to any individual, family, or community of people, service providers must learn about the culture of the specific community and the individual clients. In order to be a culturally competent therapist, one must acknowledge diversity, be sensitive to diversity, and be knowledgeable about diversity.

African Americans/Blacks

Effects of Slavery and Racism

Family: Extended, nuclear, or augmented

Serves as source of support against racism and discrimination

Serves as buffer against the stress of living

Family Roles: Interchangeable; decision making may rest with either male or female head of household

Children: Are taught to take care of their parents, and to be devoted to parents as well as to siblings

Elderly: Prized and respected

Religion: An important aspect of life; fatalistic world view—believe that life and death are predetermined; preachers have a high and respected status

Time Perception: Present orientation

Values: Family unity, loyalty, and cooperation

Work orientation

Education/achievement orientation

Cultural Themes: Strong oral tradition of storytelling

Humor, music, and dance

Actions as reflections of true feelings and sentiments

Emphasize people

Communication Style: Nonverbal: Gestures are used more; tend to look at someone (direct eye contact) when they are talking and look away (indirect eye contact) while listening; likely to nod head and make responses to indicate they are listening

Body Space: Tend to move in closer when talking.

Verbal: Public behavior may be emotionally intense, dynamic, and demonstrative; clear distinction between "argument" and "fight"; verbal abuse is not necessarily a precursor to violence. Asking personal questions of someone one has just met for the first time is seen as improper and intrusive; the use of direct questioning is seen as harassment (i.e., asking when something will be finished is seen as rushing that person to finish); use of expression "you people" is seen as pejorative and racist; silence denotes refutation of accusation (to state that you feel accused is regarded as an admission of guilt).

Support Networks: Uses both formal and kinship systems

Health Status: Life Expectancy—65 years, males; 74 years, females

Risk factors: Dietary patterns: excessive salt consumption

increased cholesterol

decreased dairy product consumption

intolerance to dairy products

obesity

Unintentional injuries: Poisoning, asphyxiation, drowning

Homicide, especially among those less than 25 years of age

Diseases: heart diseases, cancer, cerebrovascular accident (CVA), diabetes, hypertension, cirrhosis, anemia, AIDS

Health Practices/Utilization: Faith healers, root doctors, and spiritualists

Majority use modern health care facilities and systems

African American women receive less preventive health care, including prenatal care, due to poor access to services

Health Belief: The secret to good health is maintaining a balance between the forces of good and evil.

Principal Stressors:

- Frustration from continuing discrimination and rejection

- Weakening of the family support network
- Poverty and pressure of economic instability
- Weakening of traditional community and family ties which are so important in socializing children and coping with stress
- Limited or no health insurance
- Limited access to health care
- Poor health
- Feelings of rage and worthlessness that are often dealt with through self-destructive behavior—violence, drugs, alcohol abuse, suicide

Asian Americans/ Pacific Islanders

Most immigrated from another country

Predominately foreign born

Generational diversity

Family: Extended and nuclear

Patriarchal

Traditional female role

Children: Represent the future of the family; are expected to bring reputation and wealth to the extended family

Elderly: Respected and deferred to because of their wisdom

Tend to live with their children and families

Family Dynamics:

Great importance is placed on the family

Decision making is the responsibility of the total family

Shame and guilt are collectively shared by the family

Dependency and conformity are prolonged within the family

Public admission of problems is avoided

Individual Behavior:

Individual is primarily a member of the family

Avoid shame and guilt

Avoid calling attention to themselves

Expected to submerge their own behaviors and feelings

Religions:

Buddhism, Catholicism, Christianity, Confucianism, Muhammadanism, Shintoism, Taoism; belief in good and evil spirits; belief in reincarnation

Time Perception: Belief that time is flexible so there is no need to hurry or be punctual except in extremely important situations; spend hours getting to know people and view predetermined, abrupt endings as rude

Cultural Values:

High educational standards

Emotional restraint

Formality and politeness

Silent in public settings

Strong work orientation

Unquestioning respect for and deference to authority

Self-reliance, obedience

Social solidarity; respect for culture and social organizations

Harmonious interpersonal relationships

Cultural Themes:

Definite place in society/prescribed status

Needs of the family always take precedence over the needs of any given individual

Group loyalty and dependence

Continuum from past to future

Communication Styles:

Nonverbal: Women do not shake hands with each other or with men; touching of strangers is inappropriate; eye con tact between strangers is considered shameful; sometimes laugh or smile to mask other emotions or to avoid conflict

Verbal: Nonaggressive; self deprecating; nonconfrontational (to avoid confrontation, disrespect, disagreement, frustration about, or even anger, are silent or smile reluctantly); noncommunicative about personal feelings

Health Status: Life expectancy—greater than whites

Risk factors—healthier than all other ethnic groups

Diseases—heart diseases, cancer, CVA, diabetes, pneumonia/influenza

Mental illness—depression (Southeast Asian refugees); suicide (Chinese women)

Health Practices:

Healers or diviners

Concept of Yin–Yang

Hot/cold theory

Acupuncture

Herbs, ginseng, self-restraint

Mediation

Western medicine

Health Beliefs: Health depends on maintaining a balance of bodily elements

Strong emotions and improper diet can disturb this balance

Illness may result from bad conduct

Principal Stressors

- Language barrier
- Level and/or mode of adaptation to American society

Hispanic/Latino Americans

Foreign or native born

Generational diversity

Level of acculturation and assimilation

Intracultural variability and diversity

Family: Extended, nuclear, female-headed

Institution of compadrazzo (bond between a child's parents and godparents)

Family Dynamic:

Family solidarity and obligation are very important.

Traditionally prescribed roles: male—dominant authority figure, decision maker, and head of household (machismo); female—nurturer, household responsibilities, and child rearing and education (marianismo)

Elderly: Well-respected; cared for within the home

Children: Considered a priority; longer period of dependence on parents; older children are expected to consult parents for advice on important issues

Time Orientation: More concerned with the present than the future

Reputation for being late or on "Latin time" out of consideration for others who may not be ready

Religion: Strong religious beliefs; Catholicism

Cultural Values:

Spanish language

Family tie/traditional family (familism)

Folk systems

Communication:

Nonverbal: Tend to touch people with whom they are speaking; sustained direct eye contact interpreted as disrespectful or a challenge to authority; avoid direct eye contact as a sign of attentiveness and respect; tend to sit and stand close to others when engaged in conversation

Verbal: Official or business conversations are preceded by lengthy greetings, pleasantries, and other talk unrelated to the point. May have limited use and understanding of English; hesitant to disclose personal or family information to a stranger; nonconfrontational

Health Status:

Dietary practices—excessive sodium; high carbohydrates

Diseases—heart diseases, cancer, CVA, cirrhosis

Health Practices and Utilization:

Hot/cold theory

Folk practitioners

Curandero/Curamdera (uses prayer, artifacts)

Senora/Partera

Yerbero (herbalist)

Espiritisa (practitioner of Espiritism)

Santero (practitioner of Santeria)

Western medicine

Hispanic women receive less preventive health care, including prenatal care, because of limited access to services

Health Beliefs:

The secret to good health is to maintain a balance between the hot and cold humors

Fatalistic world view

There is no differentiation between physical and emotional illness

Illness has its roots in physical imbalance or supernatural forces

Principal Stressors:

* Immigration issues
* Language barrier
* Self-identity and self-acceptance
* Unemployment and poverty

Native (Indian) Americans/Alaska Natives

391 tribes living in the United States

Unique relationship with the government

Classification of "Indianness"

Urban vs reservation living

Social support is diminished and economic support is limited

Monies from land holding and/or lease provide resources for the entire family

Family: Extended (not unusual to have up to three generations in a single household)

Children: Many live under stress; experience mental health problems; and spend most of their early years in boarding schools; grandparents tend to care for younger children; many reside with foster or adoptive families off the reservation

Elderly: Reside in independent households with close contacts with children, grand children, and great grandchildren.

Family leaders

Decreased caregivers for the elderly because the adult children and relatives have often migrated to urban areas to seek employment

Cultural Values:

Tribal loyalty

Respect for elders

Reticence

Stability

Giving and sharing

Love for the land

Humility

Living in harmony with nature and peers

Appreciation of the rhythm of life

Cultural Themes:

Importance of family or clan

Honoring the tribal elders

Sacred reverence for the land and nature

Happiness as the ultimate goal

Traditional ways are the best proven ways

Communication:

Nonverbal: A bowed head is a sign of respect; gushing (making a fuss) over babies may endanger the child

Verbal: Personal questions may be considered prying; it is acceptable to ask the same question several times, if you doubt the truth of the person

Health Status:

Dietary patterns—high carbohydrates, fats, and sodium; suffer from protein deficiency

Diseases—obesity, diabetes, alcohol-related diseases, Fetal Alcohol Syndrome, unintentional injuries, cirrhosis, homicide, suicide, pneumonia, heart diseases, cancer, CVA, substance abuse, family violence

Health Practices/Utilization:

Medicine men, singing, rituals, and chants

Combination of traditional and modern medicine

Western medicine

Health Beliefs:

Attribute illness to "anger of the gods" or a sign that the person is out of harmony with nature

Principal Stressors:

- Language barrier
- Tribal variations
- Degree of acculturation
- High unemployment rate, poverty, and inadequate education
- Domestic violence and family dissolution
- Adjustment to urban living
- Stresses resulting from rapid sociocultural change, gender role changes, failed parenting skills, the changing nature of the extended family, special risks attached to boarding schools, and the relationship with the government
- Conflict between tradition and American culture

IX.

Reference List

IX. Reference List

Axelson, J. H. (1985). *Counseling and development in a multicultural society*. Pacific Grove, CA: Brooks Cole.

Blakeney, A. B. (1991). The impact of culture on patient education. *Occupational Therapy Practice, 2(3)*, 12-20.

Clark, S., & Kelley, S. D. M. (1992). Traditional Native American values: Conflict or concordance in rehabilitation? *Journal of Rehabilitation, 58*(2), 23-28.

Fitzgerald, M.H. (1992). Multicultural clinical interactions. *Journal of Rehabilitation, 58*(2), 38-42.

Jungersen, K. (1992). Culture, theory, and the practice of occupational therapy in New Zealand/Aotearoa. *American Journal of Occupational Therapy, 46*, 745-750.

Kavanagh, K. H., & Kennedy, P. H. (1992). *Promoting cultural diversity: Strategies for health care professionals*. Newbury Park: Sage.

Kluckhohn, F., & Stodtbeck, (1961). *Variations in value orientation*. Evanston, IL: Row Peterson.

Morrison, A. K. (1992). *The new leaders: Guidelines on leadership diversity in America*. San Francisco: Jossey-Bass. (Aimed at helping organization leaders develop diversity within the ranks of management.)

Skawski, K. A. (1987). Ethnic/racial considerations in occupational therapy: A survey of attitudes. *Occupational Therapy in Health Care, 4*(1), 37–48.

Smart, J. F., & Smart, D. W. (1992). Cultural issues in the rehabilitation of Hispanics. *Journal of Rehabilitation, 58*(2), 29-37.

Taylor, O. L. (1989). Clinical practice as a social occasion. In L. Cole & V. R. Deal (Eds.), *Communication disorders in multi-*

cultural populations. Rockville, MD: American Speech-Language-Hearing Association.

Thomas, R. R (1990). From affirmative action to affirming diversity. *Harvard Business Review, 90,* 107-117.

Wells, S. A. (1991). Clinical considerations in treating minority women who are disabled. *Occupational Therapy Practice, 2*(4), 13-22.

X.

Diversity and Cultural Resources

X. Diversity and Cultural Resources

Table of Contents

I. African Americans

Ahmeduzzaman, M., & Roopmarine, J. L. (1992). Sociodemographic factors, functioning style, social support and fathers' involvement with preschoolers in African-American families. *Journal of Marriage and the Family, 54,* 699-707.

Apfel, N. H., & Seitz, V. (1991). Four models of adolescent mother-grandmother relationships in black inner-city families. *Family Relations, 40,* 421-429.

Baldwin, J. (1985). *The evidence of things not seen.* New York: Henry Holt.

Barnes, A. S. (1987). *Single parents in black America: A study in culture and legitimacy.* Bristol, IN: Wyndham Hall.

Bell, D. (1987). *And we are not saved: The elusive quest for racial justice.* New York: Basic Books.

Bentley, J. (1991, February 14). The national black OT caucus. *OT Week,* pp. 10-11.

Blackwell, J. (1975). *The black community: Diversity and unity.* New York: Dodd, Mead.

Booker, S. (1991, February). Black participation in the Persian Gulf. *Jet,* pp. 4-9.

Boone, M. S. (1989). *Capital crime: Black infant mortality in America.* Newbury Parks, CA: Sage.

Bowman, P. J., & Howard, C. (1985). Race related socialization, motivation, and academic achievement: A study of black youths in three-generation families. *Journal of the American Academy of Child Psychiatry, 24,* 134-141.

Branch, T. (1988). *Parting the waters: America in the King years, 1954-63.* New York: Simon & Schuster.

Broman, C. (1991). Gender, work-family roles and psychological well-being of blacks. *Journal of Marriage and the Family, 53,* 509-520.

Buckalew, L. W., & Wynn, C. (1979). *Black American heritage: Contributions to the American culture.* Palo Alto, CA: R & E Research Associates.

Bryant, Z. L., & Coleman, M. (1988). The black family as portrayed in introductory marriage and family textbooks. *Family Relations, 37,* 255-259.

Carr, P. G., & Mednick, M. T. (1988). Sex role socialization and the development of achievement motivation in black preschool children. *Sex Roles, 18,* 169-180.

Collins, P. H. (1987). The meaning of motherhood in black culture and black mother/daughter relationships. *SAGE: A Scholarly Journal on Black Women, 4,* 3-10.

Corman, J. P. (1988). Maggie's American dream: the life and times of a black family. New York: Penguin.

Cross, W. E., Jr. (1977). Third Conference on Empirical Research in Black Psychology. Ithaca, NY: Cornell University.

Cruise, H. (1987). *Plural but equal: A critical study of Blacks and minorities and America's plural society.* New York: William Morrow.

Cutspec, P., & Goering, E. (1988). Acknowledging cultural diversity: Perceptions of shyness within the black culture. *The Howard Journal of Communications, 1,* 75-87.

Ellis, C. G. (1990). Family ties, friendships, and subjective well-being among black Americans. *Journal of Marriage and the Family, 52,* 298-310.

Farley, R., & Allen, W. (1984). *The color line and the quality of life in America.* New York Russell Sage Foundation.

Foner, E. (1988). *Reconstruction: America's unfinished revolution, 1863-1877.* New York: Harper & Row.

Franklin, J. H., & Moss, A. (1987). *From slavery to freedom: A history of Negro Americans.* New York: Knopf.

Garrow, D. J. (1986). *Bearing the cross: Martin Luther King, Jr. and the Southern Christian Leadership Conference.* New York: William Morrow.

Gages-Williams, J., Jackson, M. N., Jenkins-Monroe, V., & Williams, L. R. (1992). The business of preventing African American infant mortality. *Western Journal of Medicine, 157,* 35-356.

Gibson, R. C., & Jackson, J. S. (1987). Health, physical functioning, and informal supports of the black elderly, *Milbank Quarterly, 65,* 421-454.

Goldscheider, F. K., & Goldscheider, C. (1991). The intergenerational flow of income: Family structure and the status of black Americans. *Journal of Marriage and the Family, 53,* 499-508.

Goodwin, M. H. (1990). *He-said-she-said: Talk as social organization among black children.* Bloomington, IN: Indiana University Press.

Gray, G. (1991, February 28). Tuskegee University: Steeped in history. *OT Week,* pp. 10-11.

Hale-Benson, J. E. (1982). *Black children: Their roots, culture, and learning style.* Baltimore: Johns Hopkins University Press.

Hill, R. (1972). *The strengths of black families.* White Plains, NY: Emerson Hall.

Holton, J. (1992). African America's needs and participation in child maltreatment prevention services: Toward a community response to child abuse and neglect. *Urban Research Review, 14*(1), 1-5.

Jackson, J. (1981). Urban black Americans. In A. Harwood (Ed.), *Ethnicity and medical care* (pp. 37-129). Cambridge, MA: Harvard University Press.

Jackson, J. S. (Ed.). (1988). *The black American elderly.* New York: Springer.

Joe, B. E. (1993, February 11). Black history month: Dorothy Wilson: A role model for the profession. *OT Week,* pp. 18-19.

Joe, B. E. (1989, August 17). Black OT succeeds despite apartheid. *OT Week,* pp. 6-8.

Keith, V. M., & Smither, D. P. (1988). Current differential in black and white life expectancy. *Demography, 25,* 625-632.

King, J. (1979). African survivals in the black American family: Key factors in stability. In G. Henderson (Ed.), *Understanding counseling ethnic minorities* (pp. 43-59). Springfield, IL: Charles C Thomas.

Krause, N., & Tran, T. V. (1989). Stress and religious involvement among older blacks. *Journals of Gerontology, 44,* S4-S13.

Kuna, R. (1977). Hoodoo: The indigenous medicine and psychiatry of the black American. *Mankind Quarterly, 18,* 137-151.

Landry, B. (1987). *The new black middle class.* Berkeley: University of California Press.

Llorens, L. A. (1971). Black culture and child development. *American Journal of Occupational Therapy, 25,* 144-148.

Lowery, E. (1987). *AIDS and the black community.* Southern Christian Leadership Conference/W.O.M.E.N. Atlanta, GA: BAC Printing Co.

Manton, K. G., Patrick, C. H., & Johnson, K. W. (1987). Health differentials between blacks and whites: Recent trends in mortality and morbidity. *The Milbank Quarterly, 65,* 129-199.

Martin, E. P., & Martin, J. M. (1978). *The black extended family.* Chicago: University of Chicago Press.

McAdoo, H. P. (1988). *Black families.* Newbury Park, CA: Sage.

McAdoo, H. P., & McAdoo, J. L. (1985). *Black children: Social, educational, and parental environments.* Newbury Park, CA: Sage.

McAdoo, J. L. (Ed.). (1981). *Black families.* Beverly Hills, CA: Sage

McAdoo, J. L. (1985–1986). A black perspective on the father's role in child development. *Marriage and Family Review, 9,* 117-133.

Mitchell, H. H. (1975). Black belief: Folk beliefs of blacks in America and West Africa. New York: Harper & Row.

National Research Council. (1989). *A common destiny: Blacks and American society.* Washington, DC: Academy Press.

Neal, A. M., & Wilson, M. L. (1989). The role of skin color and feature in the black community: Implications for black women and therapy. *Clinical Psychology Review, 9,* 323-333.

Peterson, G. W., & Peters, D. F. (1985). The socialization of values of low-income Appalachian white and rural black mothers: A comparative study. *Journal of Comparative Family Studies, 16,* 75-91.

Petchers, M. K., & Milligan, S. E. (1988). Access to health care in a black urban elderly population. *Gerontologist, 28,* 213-217.

Randall-David, E. (1985). *"Mama always said": The transmission of health care beliefs among three generations of rural black women.* Unpublished doctoral dissertation, University of Florida, Gainesville.

Register, J. C. (1981). Aging and race: A black-white comparative analysis. *Gerontologist, 21,* 438-443.

Rodriguez, M. (1988). Do blacks and hispanics evaluate assertive male and female characters differently? *The Howard Journal of Communications, 1,* 101-107.

Rowland, S. E., & Wampler, K. S. (1983). Black and white mothers' preferences for parenting programs. *Family Relations Journal of Applied Family and Child Studies, 32,* 323-330.

Schab, F. (1984). Minimum competency: A comparison of reactions of southern black high school students, their parents and black teachers. *Adolescence, 19,* 107-112.

Shure, M. B. (1983). Enhancing childrearing skills in lower income women. Special issue: Social and psychological problems of women: Prevention and crisis intervention. *Issues in Mental Health Nursing, 5*(1-4), 121-138.

Sistler, A., & Gottfried, N. (1990). Shared child development knowledge between grandmother and mother. *Family Relations, 39,* 92-98.

Smallegan, M. (1989). Level of depressive symptoms and life stresses for cultural diverse older adults. *Gerontologist, 29,* 45-50.

Smerglia, V. L., Deimling, G. T., & Barresi, C. M. (1988). Black/white family comparisons in helping and decision-making networks of impaired elderly. *Family Relations, 37,* 305-309.

Smith, E. (1981). Cultural and historical perspectives in counseling blacks. In D. Sue (Ed.), *Counseling the culturally different* (pp. 141-185). New York: Wiley.

Snow, L. F. (1983). Traditional health beliefs and practices among lower class black Americans. *The Western Journal of Medicine, 139*(6), 820-828.

Spencer, M. R. (1983). Children's cultural values and parental child rearing strategies. *Developmental Review, 3,* 351-370.

Straight, W. (1983). Throw downs, fixing, rooting and hexing. *Journal of Florida Medical Association, 70,* 635-641.

Super, C. M., & Harkness, S. (1986). The developmental niche: A conceptualization at the interface of child and culture. Special issue: Cross-cultural human development. *International Journal of Behavioral Development, 9,* 545-569.

Taylor, R. J. (1990). Need for support and family involvement among black Americans. *Journal of Marriage and the Family, 52,* 584-590.

Taylor, R. J., & Chatters, L. M. (1988). Correlates of education, income and poverty among aged blacks. *Gerontologist, 28,* 435-441.

Taylor, R. J., Chatters, L. M., Tucker, M. B., & Lewis, E. (1990). Developments in research on black families: A decade review. *Journal of Marriage and the Family, 52,* 993-1014.

Tingling, D. (1967). Voodoo, rootwork, and medicine. *Psychosomatic Medicine, 29,* 483-490.

Van Sertima, I. (1983). *Blacks in science: Ancient and modern.* New Brunswick, NJ: Transaction Publishers.

Walker, J. E. (1992). Treatment of African-American clients with developmental disabilities. *Developmental Disabilities Special Interest Section Newsletter, 15*(1), 3-4.

Walter, D. (1986). AIDS in the black community. *The Advocate, 2,* 10-11, 20-21.

Weintraub, R. (1973). The influence of others: Witchcraft and root-work as explanations of behavior disturbances. *Journal of Nervous and Mental Disease, 156,* 318-326.

Wells, S. A. (1993, February 4). Black history month: A legacy of involvement. *OT Week,* pp. 18-19.

Whitten, N. E. (1986). *Black frontiersmen: Afro-Hispanic culture of Ecuador and Columbia.* Prospect Heights, IL: Waveland Press.

Wilson, M. N., Tolson, T. F. J., Himton, I. D., & Kiernan, M. (1990). Flexibility and sharing of childcare duties in black families. *Sex Roles, 22,* 409-425.

Wilson, W. J. (1987). *The truly disadvantaged: The inner city, the underclass and public policy.* Chicago: University of Chicago Press.

Zabin, L. S., Wong, R., Weinick, R. M., & Emerson, M. R. (1992). Dependency in urban black families following the birth of an adolescent's child. *Journal of Marriage and the Family, 52,* 496-507.

II. Aging

Agree, E. M. (1988). Appendix I: Portrait of Native American, Spanish, Asian and black elderly. *Hearing-Planning for aging America: The void in reliable data, October 20, 1987.* (Comm. Publ. 100-645), Washington, DC: U.S. Government Printing Office.

Anderson, N., & Cohen, H. (1989). Health status of aged minorities: Directions for clinical research. *Journal of Gerontology, 44*(1), M1-2.

Ansello, E. F. (1988). A view of aging America and some implications. *Caring, 7,* 4-7 ff.

Ansello, E. F., & Rose, T. (1989). *Aging and lifelong disabilities: Partnership for the twenty-first century.* Palm Spring, CA: Elvirita Lewis Foundation Elder Press.

Baker, F. M. (1992). Ethnic minority elders: A mental health research agenda. *Hospital and Community Psychiatry, 43,* 337-338.

Barney, K. F. (1991). From Ellis Island to assisted living: Meeting the needs of older adults from diverse cultures. *American Journal of Occupational Therapy, 45,* 586-593.

Blair, N. Y., & Leland, H. (1959). Management of the geriatric mentally retarded patient. *Mental Hospital, 9,* 9-12.

Cantor, M. (1982). The informal support system of New York's inner city elderly: Is ethnicity a factor? In D. Gelfand & A. Kutzik (Eds.), *Ethnicity and aging* (pp. 153-174). New York: Springer.

Cantor, M., & Mayer, M. (1976). Health and the inner-city elderly. *The Gerontologist, 16,* 17-26.

Carsrud, A. L., Carsrud, K. B., & Standifer, J. (1980). Social variables affecting mental health in geriatric mentally retarded individuals: An exploratory study. *Mental Retardation, 18,* 88-90.

Carter, A. (1982). Religion and the black elderly: The historical basis of social and psychological concerns. In R. Manuel (Ed.), *Minority aging: Sociological and social psychological issues* (pp. 77-93). Westport, CT: Greenwood.

Chatters, L., Taylor, R., & Jackson, J. (1985). Size and composition of the informal helper networks of elderly blacks. *Journal of Gerontology, 40,* 605-614.

Cotten, P., Sison, G., & Starr, S. (1981). Comparing elderly mentally retarded and non-mentally retarded individuals. Who are they? What are their needs? *The Gerontologist, 21,* 359-365.

Creecy, R., & Roosevelt, W. (1979). Morale and informal activity with friends among black and white elders. *The Gerontologist, 19,* 544-547.

DiGiovanni, L. (1978). The elderly retarded: A little-known group. *The Gerontologist, 18,* 262-266.

Dowd, J., & Bengtson, V. (1978). Aging in minority populations: An examination of the double jeopardy hypothesis. *Journal of Gerontology, 33,* 427-436.

Edgerton, R. B. (1988). Aging in the community—A matter of choice. *American Journal on Mental Retardation, 92,* 331-335.

Eve, S., & Friedsam, H. (1979). Ethnic differences in the use of health care among older Texans. *Journal of Minority Aging, 4,* 62-75

Federal Council on the Aging. (1990). Policy Issues Concerning the Elderly Minorities: A Staff Report, December, 1979, viii; 72 pp. Washington, DC: U. S. Department of Health and Human Services.

Ford, A., Haug, M., Jones, P., Roy, A., & Folmar, S. (1990). Race-related differences among elderly urban residents: A cohort study, 1975-1984. *Journal of Gerontology, 45,* S163-171.

Fillenbaum, G., George, L., & Palmore (1985). Determinants and consequences of retirement among men of different races and economic levels. *Journal of Gerontology, 40,* 85-94.

Heisel, M., & Faulkner, A. (1982). Religiosity in an older black population. *The Gerontologist, 22,* 354-358.

Herrera, P. M. (1983). *Innovative programming for the aging and aged mentally retarded/developmentally disabled adult.* Akron, OH: Exploration Series.

Jackson, J. (1971). Sex and social class variations in black aged parent-adult child relationships. *Aging and Human Development, 2,* 96-107.

Jackson, J. S. (1989). Race, ethnicity, and psychological theory and research. *Journal of Gerontology, 44,* 1-2.

Jackson, M., Kolody, B., & Wood, J. (1982). To be old and black: The case for double jeopardy on income and health. In R. Manuel (Ed.), *Minority aging: Sociological and social psychological issues* (pp.77-93). Westport, CT: Greenwood.

Janicki, M. P. (Ed.). (1988). Special Issue of *Mental Retardation, 46*(4).

Janicki, M., Krauss, M., & Seltzer, M. (1988). *Community residences for persons with developmental disabilities: Here to stay.* Baltimore, MD: Paul H. Brookes.

Janicki, M., & MacEachron, A. (1984). Residential, health, and social services needs of elderly developmentally disabled persons. *The Gerontologist, 24,* 128-137.

Janicki, M. P., & Wisniewski, H. N. (Eds.). (1985). Aging and developmental disabilities: Issues and approaches. Baltimore, MD: Paul H. Brookes.

Johnson, R. (1978). Barriers to adequate housing for elderly blacks. *Aging, 287-288,* 33-39.

Koening, R., Goldner, N., Kresojevich, R., & Lockwood, G. (1971). Ideas about illness of elderly blacks and whites in an urban hospital. *Aging and Human Development, 2,* 217-225.

Kraus, N., & Tran, T. (1989). Stress and religious involvement among older blacks. *Journal of Gerontology, 44,* S4-13.

Langston, E. (1980). Kith and kin: Natural support systems: Their implications for policies and programs for the black aged. *Proceedings of the National Institute on Minority Aging, 7,* 125-141.

Lavee, Y., McCubbin, H., & Olson, D. (1987). The effect of stressful life events and transitions on family functioning and well-being. *Journal of Marriage and the Family, 49,* 857-873.

Lederman, E. (1984). *Occupational therapy in mental retardation.* Springfield, IL: Charles C Thomas.

Manton, K. (1982). Differential life expectancy: Possible explanations during the later ages. In R. Manuel (Ed.), *Minority aging: Sociological and social psychological issues* (pp. 63-70). Westport, CT: Greenwood.

Manuel, R., & Reid, J. (1982). A comparative demographic profile of the minority and nonminority aged. In R. Manuel (Ed.), *Minority aging: Sociological and social psychological issues* (pp. 31-52). Westport, CT: Greenwood.

Markson, E. W. (1982). Ethnicity as a factor in the institutionalization of the ethnic elderly. In D. Gelfand & A. Kutzik (Eds.), *Ethnicity and aging* (pp. 341-356). New York: Springer.

McCree, S. (1989). Sensitivity to the black elderly client. *Gerontology Special Interest Section Newsletter, 12*(3), 1-2.

McCubbin, H., Joy, C., Cauble, A., Comeau, Patterson, J., & Needle, R. (1980, November). Family stress and coping: A decade review. *Journal of Marriage and the Family,* 855-871.

McNeely, R. L., & Colen, J. N. (1983). *Aging in minority groups.* Newbury Park, CA: Sage.

Mindel, C., Roosevelt, W., & Richard, S. (1986). Informal and formal health and social support systems of black and white elderly: A comparative cost approach. *The Gerontologist, 26,* 279-285.

Miranda, M., & Ruiz, R. A. (Eds.). (1981). Chicano Aging and Mental Health, x; 270 p. Rockville, MD: U.S. Department of Health and Human Services, Public Health Service, Alcohol, Drug Abuse, and Mental Health Administration, National Institute of Mental Health.

Morrison, B. (1983). Sociocultural dimensions: Nursing homes and the minority aged. In G. S. Getzel & M. J. Meller (Eds.), *Gerontological social work practice in long-term care* (pp. 127-145). Binghamton, NY: Haworth Press.

Mutran, E. (1985). Intergenerational family support among blacks and whites: Response to culture or to socioeconomic differences. *Journal of Gerontology, 40,* 382-389.

White House Conference on Aging. (1981). *Report of mini-conference on Pacific/Asian Elderly "Pacific/Asians the wisdom of age."* Washington, DC: White House Conference on Aging.

White House Conference on Aging. (1981). *Report of mini-conference on Hispanic aging.* Washington, DC: White House Conference on Aging.

White House Conference on Aging. (1981). *Report of mini-conference on Euro-American elderly.* Washington, DC: White House Conference on Aging.

White House Conference on Aging. (1981). *Report of mini-conference on Pacific Islanders jurisdiction.* Washington, DC: White House Conference on Aging.

White House Conference on Aging. (1981). *Report of mini-conference on the American Indian/Alaskan Native elderly.* Washington, DC: White House Conference on Aging.

Petcher, K., & Milligan, S. (1988). Access to health care in a black urban elderly population. *The Gerontologist, 28,* 213-217.

Raphael, E. I. (1988). Grandparents: A study of their role in hispanic families. *Physical & Occupational Therapy in Geriatrics, 6,* 31-62.

Register, J. (1981). Aging and race: A black-white comparative analysis. *The Gerontologist, 21,* 438-443.

Richardson, V., & Kitty, K. (1989). Retirement financial planning among black professionals. *The Gerontologist, 29,* 32-37.

Smallegan, M. (1989). Level of depressive symptoms and life stresses for culturally diverse older adults. *The Gerontologist, 29,* 45-50.

Seltzer, M. M., & Krauss, M. W. (1987). *Aging and mental retardation: Extending the continuum of the American association on Mental Retardation.* [Monographs] Washington, DC: American Association on Mental Retardation.

Seltzer, M., Krauss, M., Litchfield, L., & Modlish, N. (1989). Utilization of aging network services by elderly persons with mental retardation. *The Gerontologist, 29,* 234-238.

Seltzer, M., & Seltzer, G. (1985). The elderly mentally retarded: A group in need of service. *Journal of Gerontological Social Work, 8,* 99-119.

Shapiro, M. A. (1985). Use of time and morale in women of advanced aged. Los Angeles: University of Southern California.

Smerglia, V., Deimling, G., & Barresi, C. (1988). Black/white family comparisons in helping and decision-making networks of impaired elderly. *Family Relations, 37,* 305-309.

Stanford, P. (1979). Minority aging research project. *Gerontology Special Interest Section Newsletter, 2,* 3.

Stroud, M., Roberts, R., & Murphy, M. D. (1987). Life status of elderly mentally retarded/developmentally disabled persons. In J. M. Berg & J. M. Dejong (Eds.), *Science and service in mental retardation: Proceedings of the Seventh Congress of the International Association for the Scientific Study of Mental Deficiency.* (1st ed.) (pp 317-334). Routledge Chapman & Hall.

Stroud, M., & Sutton, E. (1988). *Activities handbook & instructor's guide for expanding options for older adults with developmental disabilities.* Baltimore: Paul H. Brookes.

Taylor, J., & Taylor, W. (1982). The social and economic status of the black elderly. *Phylon, 43,* 295-306.

Taylor, R. (1986). Religious participation among elderly blacks. *The Gerontologist, 26,* 630-636.

Taylor, R., & Chatters, L. (1986). Church-based informal support among elderly blacks. *The Gerontologist, 26,* 637-642.

Taylor, S. (1982). Mental health and successful coping among aged black women. In R. Manuel (Ed.), *Minority aging: Sociological and social psychological issues* (pp. 95-100). Westport, Ct: Greenwood.

Thurmond, G., & Becher, J. Jr. (1981). Dimensions of disengagement among black and white rural elderly. *International Journal of Aging and Human Development, 12,* 245-266.

U. S. Department of Commerce, Bureau of the Census. (1980). *We the black Americans.* Washington, DC: U.S. Government Printing Office.

Usui, W., Keil, T., & Phillips, D. (1983). Determinants of life satisfaction: A note on a race-interaction hypothesis. *Journal of Gerontology, 38,* 107-110.

Wallace, E. (1980). Retirement income for the black elderly. *Proceedings from the National Institute on Minority Aging, 7,* 25-27.

Walz, T., Harper, D., & Wilson, J. (1986). The aging developmentally disabled person: Review. *The Gerontologist, 26,* 622-629.

Watson, W. (1982). Mental health of the minority aged: Selected correlates. In. R. Manuel (Ed.), Minority aging: Sociological and social psychological issues (pp. 83-88). Westport, CT: Greenwood.

Wells, S. A. (1992, December 3). Issues in minority affairs: Aging among minority populations. *OT Week,* p. 7.

Yee, B. (1989). *Variations in aging: Older minorities.* Galveston, TX: The Texas Consortium of geriatric education centers: University of Texas Medical Branch at Galveston.

III. Asian Americans and Pacific Islanders

Ahearn, F. L., & Athey, J. L. (1991). *Refugee children: Theory, research, and services.* Baltimore: John Hopkins University Press.

Alkire, W. (1977). *An introduction to the peoples and cultures of Micronesia.* Menlo Park, CA: Cummings.

Allison, A. (1991, October). Japanese mothers and "obentos": The lunch-box as ideological state apparatus. *Anthropological Quarterly, 64,* 195-208.

Bellwood, P. (1987). *The Polynesians, prehistory of an island people.* New York: Thames and Hudson.

Booth, R. (1985). The two Samoas, still coming of age. *National Geographic, 168,* 452-473.

Center for Applied Linguistics. (1981). *The peoples and cultures of Cambodia, Laos, and Vietnam.* Washington, DC: Author.

Chan, S. (1986). *This bittersweet soil: The Chinese in California agriculture, 1860-1910.* Berkeley: University of California Press.

Chen, E. (1978). *The elder Chinese.* San Diego, CA: Campanile Press.

Chiu, L. H. (1987). Child-rearing attitudes of Chinese, Chinese-American and Anglo-American mothers. *International Journal of Psychology, 22,* 409-419.

Choy, B. Y. (1979). *Koreans in America.* Rutland, VA: C. E. Tuttle.

Colletta, N. (1980). *American schools for the natives of Ponape: A study of education and culture change in Micronesia.* Honolulu: University of Hawaii Press.

Commission on Wartime Relocation and Internment of Civilians. (1982). *Personal justice denied.* Brooklyn, NY: Revisionist Press.

Connolly, B., & Anderson, R. (1987). *First contact.* New York: Viking.

Cormak, A. (1974). *Chinese birthdays, weddings, funerals and other customs.* Taipei: Ch'eng Wen Publishing.

_____ (1983). *Cyclopedia of Samoa, Tonga, Tahiti, and the Cook Islands.* Papakura, New Zealand: R. McMillian.

Daniels, R. (1988). *Asian American: Chinese and Japanese in the U.S. since 1850.* Seattle: University of Washington Press.

Daws, G. (1974). *Shoal of time. A history of the Hawaiian Islands.* Honolulu: University of Hawaii Press.

Delassus, J. F. (1972). *The Japanese: A critical evaluation of the character and culture of a people.* New York: Hart.

Die, A. H., & Seelbach, W. C. (1988). Problems, sources of assistance and knowledge of services among elderly Vietnamese immigrants. *Gerontologist, 28,* 448-452.

Drinnon, R. (1987). *Keeper of concentration camps: Dillon S. Myer and American racism.* Berkeley: University of California Press.

Duphiney, L. (1972). *Oriental-Americans: An annotated bibliography.* Washington, DC: Office of Education. (ERIC Document Reproduction Service No. ED 060136).

Fleming, K. (1987). New Zealand: The last utopia? *National Geographic, 171,* 655-681.

Forrest, D. V. (1982). The eye in the heart: Psychoanalytic keys to Vietnam. *Journal of Psychoanalytic Anthropology, 5,* 259-298.

Fuller, J. (1986). *Health and social beliefs of one Vietnamese-American family.* Unpublished manuscript, University of Florida, College of Nursing.

Gallimore, R., Boggs, J. W., & Jordon, C. (1974). *Culture, behavior and education: A study of Hawaiian-Americans.* Beverly Hills, CA: Sage.

Gerstle, D., & Raitt, H. (1974). *Tonga pictorial.* San Diego, CA: Tofua Press.

Gregerson, M., & Thomas, D. (Eds.). (1980). *Notes from Indochina on ethnic minority cultures.* Dallas: Sil Museum of Anthropology.

Hawthorne, L. (1982). *Refugee: The Vietnamese experience.* New York: Oxford University Press.

Hendricks, G. L., et al. (Eds.). (1986). *The Hmong in the transition.* Staten Island, NY: Center for Migration Studies.

Herman, M. (1974). *The Japanese in America: 1843-1973.* Dobbs Ferry, NY: Oceana Publications.

Hoi, D. T., & Oliver, M. (1975). *Vietnamese culture, a slide-cassette presentation.* Washington, DC: Smart Associates.

Holmes, L. (1987). *Quest for the real Samoa: The Mead/Freeman controversy and beyond.* South Hadley, MA: Bergin and Garvey.

Hulme, K. (1983). *The bone people.* New York: Viking Penguin.

Ichioka, Y. (1988). *The issue: The world of the first generation Japanese immigrants, 1885–1924.* New York: Free Press.

Irons, P., & Drinnon, R. (1983). *Justice at war: The story of the Japanese internment cases.* New York: Oxford University Press.

Ishikawa, W. H. (1978). *The elder Guamanian.* San Diego, CA: Campanile.

Ishikawa, W. H. (1978). *The elder Samoan.* San Diego, CA: Campanile.

Ishizuka, K. C. (1978). *The elder Japanese.* San Diego, CA: Campanile.

Kay, R. (1985). *Tahiti and French Polynesia.* Berkeley, CA: Lonely Planet.

Khoa, L. X., Phan, D. T., Doeung, H. H., Chaw, K., Pham, P. G., Bounthinh, T., Vandeusen, J., & Miller, B. Southeast Asian social and cultural customs: Similarities and differences. *Journal of Refugee Resettlement, 27-46.*

Khoa, L. X., & Vandeusen, J. Social and cultural customs: Their contribution to resettlement. *Journal of Refugee Resettlement, 48-52.*

Kim, I. (1981). *New urban immigrants: The Korean community in New York.* Princeton, NJ: Princeton University Press.

Kitano, H. H. (1977). *Japanese Americans: The evolution of a sub-culture.* Englewood Cliffs, NJ: Prentice-Hall.

Kittelson, D. J. (1985). *The Hawaiians: An annotated bibliography.* Honolulu: Social Science Research Institute, University of Hawaii.

Koh, Y. K., & Bell, W. G. (1987). Korean elders in the United States: Intergenerational relations and living arrangements. *Gerontologist, 27,* 66-71.

Kroeber, A. L. (1973). *Peoples of the Philippines.* Westport, CT: Greenwood.

Kwong, P. (1979). *Chinatown NY: Labor and politics, 1930-1950.* New York: Monthly Review Press.

Kwong, P. (1988). *The new Chinatown.* New York: Hill & Wang.

Lind, A. W. (1989). *Hawaii's people.* Honolulu: University of Hawaii Press.

Lueras, L. (Ed.). (1986). *Hawaii: Insight guides.* Englewood Cliffs, NJ: Prentice Hall.

Lyman, S. M. (Ed.). (1977). *The Asian in North America.* Santa Barbara, CA: ABC-Clio Books.

Lyndon, S. (1985). *Chinese gold: The Chinese in the Monterey Bay region.* Capitola, CA: Capitola.

McDermott, J. F. (1984). Cultural variations in family attitudes and their implications for therapy. *Annual Progress in Child Psychiatry and Child Development, 145-154.*

McDermott, J., Tseng, W., & Maretzki, T. (1984). *People and cultures of Hawaii: A psychocultural profile.* Honolulu: University of Hawaii Press.

McKenzie, J., & Chrisman, N. (1977). Healing herbs, gods, and magic: Folk health beliefs among Filipino-Americans. *Nursing Outlook, 25,* 326-329.

Mead, M. (1975). *New lives for old.* New York: Morrow Quill Paperbacks.

Melendy, H. B. (1977). *Asians in America: Filipinos, Koreans and East Indians.* Boston, MA: Twayne.

Meyers, C. (1992). Hmong children and their families: Consideration of cultural influences in assessment. *American Journal of Occupational Therapy, 46,* 737-744.

Morrow, R. D. (1987). Cultural differences—Be aware. *Academic Therapy, 23,* 143-149.

Nakano, A. (1983). *Broken canoe: Conversations and observations in Micronesia.* Portland, OR: University of Queensland Press.

Nee, V. G, & De Barry, B. (1974). *Longtime Californ': A documentary study of an American Chinatown.* Stanford, CA: Stanford University Press.

O'Hare, W. (1990). A new look at Asian Americans. *American Demographics, 12,* 26-31.

Ohmuki-Tierney, E. (1984). *Illness and culture in contemporary Japan: An anthropological view.* New York: Cambridge University Press.

Osako, M., & Liu, W. (1986). Intergenerational relations and the aged among Japanese Americans. *Research on Aging, 8,* 128-155.

Patterson, C. (1986). At the birth of nations. *National Geographic, 170,* 460-499.

Patterson, W. (1988). *Korean frontier in America: Immigration to Hawaii, 1896-1910.* Honolulu: University of Hawaii Press.

Peterson, R. (1978). *The elder Philipino.* San Diego, CA: Campanile.

Pido, A. J. S. (1986). *The Philipinos in America: Macro/micro dimensions of immigration and integration.* Staten Island, NY: Center for Migration Studies.

Reaissland, N., & Burghart, R. (1987). The role of massage in south Asia: Child health and development. *Social Science and Medicine, 25,* 231-239.

Rebano, J. (1971). *Culture and behavior in Hawaii: An annotated bibliography.* Honolulu: Social Science Research Institute, University of Hawaii.

Reischauer, E. O. (1977). *The Japanese.* Cambridge, MA: The Belknap Press of Harvard Press.

Reischauer, E. (1988). *The Japanese today.* Cambridge, MA: Harvard University Press.

Rodman, M. (1983). *The pacification of Melanesia.* Lanham, MD: University Press of America.

Ronck, R. (Ed.). (1984). *Ronck's Hawaiian almanac.* Honolulu: University of Hawaii Press.

Rosenberg, J. A. (1986). Health care for Cambodian children: Integrating treatment plans. *Pediatric Nursing, 12,* 118-125.

Salmond, A. (1983). The study of traditional Maori society: The state of the art. *The Journal of the Polynesian Society, 92,* 309-331.

Saito, S. (1972). *Philippine ethnography: A critically annotated and selected bibliography.* Honolulu: University Press of Hawaii.

Santopietro, M. C. S., & Smith, C. (1981). Indochina moves to main street: How to get through to a refugee patient. *RN Magazine, 44*(1), 43-48.

Sata, L. S. (1977). Musings of a hyphenated American. In S. Sue & N. M. Wagner (Eds.), *Asian Americans: Psychological perspectives.* Ben Lomond, CA: Science & Behavior Books.

Sih, K. T., & Allen, L. B. (1976). *The Chinese in America.* New York: Arno.

Soohoo, D. (1982). *Comparison of Asian-American, European-American, and Denver infants at 24 months on the Denver developmental screening test.* Los Angeles: University of Southern California.

Spadone, R. A. (1992). Internal-external control and temporal orientation among southeast Asians and white Americans. *American Journal of Occupational Therapy, 46,* 713-719.

Strand, P. J., & Jones, W., Jr. (1985). *Indochina refugees in America: Problems of adaptation and assimilation.* Durham, NC: Duke University Press.

Strom, R., Park, S. H., & Daniels, S. (1987). Childrearing dilemmas of Korean immigrants to the United States. *Scientia Paedagogica Experimentalis, 24,* 91-102.

Sue, D. (1981). Cultural and historical perspectives in counseling Asian Americans. In D. Sue (Ed.), *Counseling the culturally different: Theory and practice* (pp. 113-140). New York: Wiley.

Synder, P. (1984). Health service implications of folk healing among older Asian Americans and Hawaiians in Honolulu. *Gerontologist, 24,* 471-476.

Takaki, R. (1989). *Strangers from a different shore: A history of Asian Americans.* Boston: Little, Brown.

Thomas, S. (1987). The last navigator. New York: Henry Holt.

Toupin, E., & Ahn, S. W. (1980). Counseling Asians: Psychotherapy in the context of racism and Asian-American history. *American Journal of Orthopsychiatry, 50,* 76-86.

Tsai, S. (1983). *China and the overseas Chinese in the U.S., 1868-1911.* Fayetteville, AZ: University of Arkansas Press.

Vandeusen, J., Coleman, C., Khoa, L. X., Phan, D., Chaw, H., Nguyen, L. T., Pham, P., & Bounthinh, T. Southeast Asian social and cultural customs: Similarities and differences. Part 1. *Journal of Refugee Resettlement,* 20-39.

Wagner, N. N. (1977). Filipinos: A minority within a minority. In S. Sue & N. N. Wagner (Eds.), *Asian Americans: Psychological perspectives.* Ben Lomond, CA: Science and Behavior Books.

Weglyn, M. (1976). *Years of infamy: The untold story of America's concentration camps.* New York: Morrow.

Wei, T. D. (1983). The Vietnamese refugee child: Understanding cultural differences. In D. R. Omark & J. G. Erickson (Eds.), *The bilingual exceptional child.* San Diego, CA: College-Hill.

Weisz, J. R., Suwanlert, S., Chaiyasit, W., & Weiss, B. (1988). Thai and American perspectives on over- and undercontrolled child behavior problems: Exploring the threshold model among parents, teachers, and psychologists. *Journal of Consulting and Clinical Psychology, 56,* 601-609.

Wheeler, T. (1986). *Rarotonga and the Cook Islands.* Berkeley, CA: Lonely Planet.

Winslow, J. (1977). *The Melanesian environment.* Canberra, Australia: Australian National University Press.

Woodson, R. H., & da Costa-Woodson, E. M. (1984). Social organization, physical environment, and infant-caretaker interaction. *Developmental Psychology, 20,* 473-476.

Wright, R. (1987). *On Fiji Islands.* Auckland, New Zealand: Penguin.

Yee, B. W. K. (in press). Loss of one's homeland and culture during the middle years. In R. A. Kalish (Ed.), *Coping with losses of middle age.* Newbury Park, CA: Sage.

Yee, B. W. K., & Van Arsdale, P. (1986). Adaptation and coping of Vietnamese elderly women: Review, research, and speculation. *High Plains Applied Anthropologist, 6,* 11-17.

Yu, L. C., & Harburg, E. (1981). Filial responsibility to aged parent: Stress of Chinese Americans. *International Journal of Group Tensions, 11*(1-4), 47-58.

IV. Assessment

Azibo, D. A. (1988). Personality, clinical, and social psychological research on blacks: Appropriate and inappropriate frameworks. *Western Journal of Black Studies, 12,* 220-233.

Agar, M. H. (1986). Speaking of ethnography. *Qualitative Research Methods Series, 2,* 79.

Bates, P. S. (1992). *Cultural differences in relating to electronic adaptive equipment: Occupational therapists, engineers, per-*

sons with spinal cord injury. Denton, TX: Texas Woman's University.

Blakeney, A. B. (1991). The impact of culture on patient education. *Occupational Therapy Practice, 2,* 12-20.

Brockett, M. M. (1987). Cultural variations in bay area functional performance evaluation scores—Considerations for occupational therapy. *The Canadian Journal of Occupational Therapy, 54,* 195-199.

Cusick, A., & Harai, H. (1991). The Allen tests for cognitive disability: Cross cultural pilot study. *Occupational Therapy in Mental Health, 11*(4), 61-75.

Dean's Grant Project, University of Kentucky. (1981). Toward a research base for the least restrictive environment: Collection of papers. *Reports of the Dean's Grants, 3,* 167.

Demars, P. A. (1992). An occupational therapy life skills curriculum model for a Native American tribe: Health promotion program based on ethnographic field research. *American Journal of Occupational Therapy, 46,* 727-736.

Egan, M. (1992, August 20). Focus: Cultural diversity: Treatment that respects cultural heritage. *OT Week,* pp. 14-15.

Evans, J., & Salim, A. A. (1992). A cross-cultural test of the validity of occupational assessments with patients with schizophrenia. *American Journal of Occupational Therapy, 46,* 685-695.

Fisher, A. G., Liu, Y., Velozo, C. A., & Pan, A. W. (1992). Cross-cultural assessment of process skills. *American Journal of Occupational Therapy, 46,* 876-885.

Frank, G., Huecker, H., Segal, R., Forwell, S., & Bagatell, N. (1991). Assessment and treatment of a pediatric patient in chronic care: Ethnographic method applied to OT practice. *American Journal of Occupational Therapy, 45,* 252-263.

Haase, B. (1992). Appropriate technology. *Developmental Disabilities Special Interest Section Newsletter, 15,* 4.

Hector, M. (1978). Importance of cultural differences on patient attitude towards treatment. *World Federation of Occupational Therapists Bulletin, 2,* 15-21.

Kinebanian, A. (1992). Cross-cultural occupational therapy: A critical reflection. *American Journal of Occupational Therapy, 46,* 751-757.

Krefting, L. (1991). The culture concept in the everyday practice of occupational and physical therapy. *Physical & Occupational Therapy in Pediatrics, 11,* 1-16.

Lange, B. K. (1988). Ethnographic interview: An occupational therapy needs assessment tool for American Indian and Alaska native alcoholics. *Occupational Therapy in Mental Health, 8,* 61-80.

Levine, R. E. (1984). The cultural aspects of home care delivery. *American Journal of Occupational Therapy, 38,* 734-738.

Litterst, T. A. E. (1985). The foundation: A reappraisal of anthropological fieldwork methods and the concept of culture in occupational therapy research. *American Journal of Occupational Therapy, 39,* 602-604.

Martin, R. M. (1986). *A study of black preschool children's performance on the Miller assessment for preschoolers.* Richmond, VA: Chesterfield School System.

Research Resources Information Center. (1984). *Minority biomedical research support program: A research resources directory.* Rockville, MD: U.S. Department of Health and Human Services, Public Health Services, National Institutes of Health.

Saeki, K., Clark, F. A., & Azen, S. P. (1985). Performance of Japanese and Japanese-American children on the motor accuracy-revised and design copying tests of the southern California sensory integration tests. *American Journal of Occupational Therapy, 39,* 103-109.

Vilaubi, A. (1990, December 13). Cultural influences: Rehabilitation treatment & outcome. *OT Week,* pp. 4-5.

Westbrook, M. T., Skropeta, C. M., & Legge, V. (1991, March). Ethnic clients in diversional therapy programs. *Australian Journal of Occupational Therapy , 38,* 251-258.

V. Disability

Hall, E. T. (1959). *The silent language.* Greenwich, CT: Fawcett.

Koestler, F. A. (1976). *The unseen minority: A social history of blindness in America.* New York: David McKay.

Kohl, H. (1990). Speechless occupational therapy. *British Journal of Occupational Therapy, 53,* 98-100.

McCuaig, M., & Frank, G. (1991). The able self: Adaptive patterns and choices in independent living for a person with cerebral palsy. *American Journal of Occupational Therapy, 45,* 224-234.

National Council on Disability. (1993). *Meeting the unique needs of minorities with disabilities: A Report to the President and the Congress.* Washington, D.C.

OSERS News in Print. (1991). *Disability and people from minority backgrounds, 3*(4).

Pandit, A. (1986). Day care of mentally handicapped people: Why is it an issue? *British Journal of Occupational Therapy, 49,* 126-129.

Spencer, J. C. (1991). An ethnographic study of independent living alternatives. *American Journal of Occupational Therapy, 45,* 243-251.

Walker, S., Belgrave, F., Nicholls, R., & Turner, K. (1991). *Future frontiers in the employment of minority persons with disabilities.* Proceeding of the National Conference of the President's Committee on Employment of People with Disabilities and the Howard University Research and Training Center for Access to Rehabilitation and Economic Opportunity, Washington, DC.

Wells, S. A. (1992, December 17). Issues in minority affairs: The other minority. *OT Week,* p. 7.

Wells, S. A. (1991). Clinical considerations in treating minority women who are disabled. *Occupational Therapy Practice, 2,* 13-22.

VI. Education

_____(1992). Issues on the education of African-American youth in special education settings [Special Issue]. *Exceptional Children, 59.*

Hamlin, R. B. (1992). Diversity education in occupational therapy. *Education Special Interest Section Newsletter, 2,* 2-3.

Heller, K. A., Holtzman, W. H., & Messick, S. (1982). *Placing children in special education: A strategy for equity.* Washington, DC: National Academy Press.

Jamison, M. (1985). The interaction of culture and learning: Implications for occupational therapy. *Canadian Journal of Occupational Therapy, 52,* 5-9.

Landes, R. (1965). *Culture in American education: Anthropological approaches to minority and dominant groups in the schools.* New York: Wiley.

Locke, D. C. (1989). Fostering the self-esteem of African American children. *Elementary School Guidance & Counseling, 23,* 254-259.

Magary, J. F., Buscaqlia, L. F., & Light, B. (1968). Sixth annual distinguished lectures in special education and rehabilitation, summer session 1967. *Distinguished Lecture Series, Sixth Annual.* Los Angeles: University of Southern California.

Riese, H. P. (1962). *Heal the hurt child: An approach through educational therapy with special reference to the extremely deprived negro child.* Chicago: University of Chicago Press.

SECON, Inc., Haynes, M. A., King, R. C., & Jenkins, W. C. *Minorities, schools of public health agencies.* Hyattsville, MD: Department of Health, Education, and Welfare.

Sayles-Folks, S. (1990, December 13). University curriculum includes cultural sensitivity training. *OT Week,* pp. 8-9.

Sayles-Folks, S., & People, L. (1990). Cultural sensitivity training for occupational therapists. *Physical Disabilities Special Interest Section Newsletter, 13,* 4-5.

U.S. Department of Health, Education, and Welfare. (1977). *An exploratory evaluation of U.S. medical schools' efforts to achieve equal representation of minority students.* Washington, DC: Author.

Vilaubi, A. (1992, October 22). Minority issues: Education must become our national priority. *OT Week,* p. 6.

VII. External Resources

American Indian Rehabilitation Research and Training Center Institute for Human Development, Arizona University Affiliated Program, PO Box 5630, Flagstaff, AZ 86011; (602) 523-4791.

The American Institute for Managing Diversity, Inc., PO Box 38, 830 Westview Dr., S.W., Atlanta, GA 30314; (404) 524-7316.

Asian American Community Mental Health Training Center, 1300 W. Olympic Boulevard, #303, Los Angeles, CA 90015; (213) 385-1474.

Asian American Psychological Association, 16591 Melville Circle, Huntington Beach, CA 92649; (213) 592-3227.

Association of American Indian Affairs, Inc., 432 Park Avenue South, New York, NY 10016; (212) 689-8720.

Association of Asian/Pacific Community Health Organizations, 3100 8th Street, Suite 210, Oakland, CA 94607; (415) 272-9536.

BEBASHI (Blacks Educating Blacks About Sexual Health Issues), 1319 Locust Street, Philadelphia, PA 19107; (215) 546-4140.

COSSMHO (Coalition of Hispanic Health and Human Service Organizations), 1030 15th Street, NW, Washington, DC 20005; (202) 371-2100.

Health Education Resource Organization (HERO), 101 West Read Street, Suite 812, Baltimore, MD 21201; (301) 685-1180.

The International Society of Intercultural Education, Training, and Research (SIETAR), 733 15th St., NW, Suite 900, Washington, DC 20005; (202) 737-5000.

Japanese American Citizens League, National Headquarters, 1765 Sutter Street, San Francisco, CA 94115; (415) 921-5225.

The Kupona Network, 4611 South Ellis Avenue, Chicago, IL 60653; (312) 536-3000.

Multicultural Prevention Resource Center (MPRC), 1540 Market Street, Suite 320, San Francisco, CA 94102; (415) 861-2142.

National Association for the Advancement of Colored People (NAACP), 1790 Broadway, New York, NY 10019; (212) 245-2100.

National Association For Black Psychologists, 1125 Spring Road, NW, Washington, DC 20010; (202) 576-7184.

National Black Women's Health Project, 1217 Gordon Street, SW, Atlanta, GA 30810; (404) 753-0919.

National Center for Urban Ethnic Affairs, 1521 16th Street, NW, Washington, DC 20036; (202) 232-3600.

National Conference of Puerto Rican Women, PO Box 4804, Washington, DC 20012; (202) 387-4716.

National Congress on American Indians/NCAI Fund, 1430 K Street, NW, Suite 700, Washington, DC 20005; (202) 347-9520.

National Council of La Raza, 810 First Street, NE, Suite 300, Washington, DC 20002; (202) 289-1380.

National Urban League, 500 E. 62nd Street, New York, NY 10021; (212) 310-9000.

Office of Latino Affairs, 2000 14th Street, NW, 2nd Floor, Washington, DC 20009; (202) 347-0390.

Office of Minority Health, Dept. of Health & Human Services, 200 Independence Avenue, SW, Room 118F, Washington, DC 20201; (202) 245-0020.

Office of Minority Health Resource Center, PO Box 37337, Washington, DC, 20013-7337; (301) 587-1938.

OSERS News in Print, U.S. Dept. of Education, Office of Special Education and Rehabilitative Services, 330 C Street, SW, Switzer Building Rm 3129, Washington, DC 20202-2524; (202) 732-1723.

VIII. Gender

Brown, K., & Gillespie, D. (1992). Recovering relationships: A feminist analysis of recovery models. *American Journal of Occupational Therapy, 46,* 1001-1005.

IX. General

Alba, R. D. (1990). *Ethnic identity: The transformation of white America.* New Haven, CT: Yale University Press.

Barney, K. (1989). Cultural awareness perspectives—Introduction. *Gerontology Special Interest Section Newsletter, 12*(2), 1-2.

Barney, K. (1989). Cultural sensitivity issues, Part II—Introduction. *Gerontology Special Interest Section Newsletter, 12*(3), 1.

Beynon, S. (1992). Stranger in a strange land: A consumer guide to occupational therapy. *British Journal of Occupational Therapy, 55,* 186-188.

Breer, P. E., & Locke, E. A. (1965). *Task experience as a source of attitudes.* Homewood, IL: Dorsey.

Brown, I. C. (1963). Understanding other cultures. Englewood Cliffs, NJ: Prentice Hall.

Burke, J. P. (1975). *A model of occupational behavior: The evolution of role, personal, causation and socialization.* Los Angeles: University of Southern California.

Calhoun, D. W. (1981). *Sports, culture & personality.* Champaign, IL: Leisure Press.

Chang, F. T. (1989). *The study of fine motor coordination and cognitive functions in adults from two cultures: American and Chinese.* Philadelphia: Temple University.

Clark, A. L. (1981). *Culture and childrearing.* Philadelphia: F. A. Davis.

Cohen, Y. A. (Ed.). (1971). *Man in adaptation: The institutional framework.* Chicago: Aldine.

Creative partnerships: Minority recruitment in Philadelphia. (1988). *Occupational Therapy News, 42*(3), 1, 16.

Dyck, I. (1989). The immigrant client: Issues in developing culturally sensitive practice. *Canadian Journal of Occupational Therapy, 56,* 248-255.

Dyck, I. (1991). National perspective: Multiculturalism and occupational therapy: Sharing the challenge. *Canadian Journal of Occupational Therapy, 58,* 224-226.

Esman, A. (1990). *Adolescence and culture.* New York: Columbia University Press.

Evans, J. (1992). Nationally speaking: what occupational therapists can do to eliminate racial barriers to health care access. *American Journal of Occupational Therapy, 46,* 679-683.

Freedman, D. G. (1979, January). Ethnic differences in babies. *Human Nature.*

Gibbs, B. K. (1990, October 18). A challenge to minority practitioners. *OT Week.* pp. 10, 42.

Gibbs, B. K. (1991). Cultural diversity: Our responsibility for the future. *Administration & Management Special Interest Section Newsletter, 7*(2), 1-3.

Gibbs, B. K. (1991, February 28). Focus: Staffing: Staffing for diversity. *OT Week,* pp. 8, 16.

Gfellner, B. M. (1990). Culture and consistency in ideal and actual child-rearing practices: A study of Canadian Indian and white parents. *Journal of Comparative Family Studies, 21*, 413-423.

Hatch, E. (1973). *Theories of man and culture.* New York: Columbia University Press.

Hinojosa, J. (1992). Defining multiculturalism. *Education Special Interest Section Newsletter, 2*(4), 1-2.

Jahoda, G., & Lewis, I. M. (Eds.). (1989). *Acquiring culture: Cross cultural studies in child development.* London: Routledge.

Joe, B. E. (1990, December 13). Serving the undeserved. *OT Week,* pp. 28-29.

Joe, B. E. (1991, August 15). Tackling the minority personnel shortage. *OT Week,* p. 8.

Johnson, J. A. (1985). Wellness: Its myths, realities, and potential for occupational therapy. *Occupational Therapy in Health Care, 2,* 117-138.

Kephart, W., & Jedlicka, D. (1988). The family society and the individual. New York: Harper & Row.

Kilbride, P. L., Goodale, J.C., & Ameisen, E. R. (1990). *Encounters with American ethnic cultures.* Tuscaloosa: University of Alabama Press.

Kotlowitz, A. (1991). There are no children here: The story of two boys growing up in the other America. New York: Anchor Books/Doubleday.

Klavins, R. (1972). Work-play behavior: Cultural influences: The relevance of work-play theory to human adaptation. *American Journal of Occupational Therapy, 26,* 176-179.

Klavins, R. (1969). *An inventory of cultural value orientations.* Los Angeles: University of Southern California.

Kramer, P. (1992). From the editor. *Education Special Interest Section Newsletter, 2*(4), 1.

Krefting, L., & Krefting, D. (1991). Leisure activities after a stroke: An ethnographic approach. *American Journal of Occupational Therapy, 45,* 429–436.

Landale, N. S., & Guest, A. M. (1990). Generation, ethnicity, and occupational opportunity in late 19th century America. *American Sociological Review, 55,* 280-296.

Latest recruitment effort targets African-Americans. (1992, June 11). *OT Week,* p. 15.

Laumann, E. D. (1973). Bonds of pluralism: *The form and substance of urban social networks.* New York: Wiley.

Levinson, D. (1989). *Family violence in cross-cultural perspective.* Newbury Park, CA: Sage.

Lowery, C. (1990). Uncovering cultural bias and coping with it. *Physical Disabilities Special Interest Section Newsletter, 13,* 2-3.

Mannheim, K. (1982). *Structures of thinking.* Boston: Routledge & Kegan Paul.

Marjoribanks, K. (1992). Ethnicity, families as opportunity structures and adolescents' aspirations. *Ethnic and Racial Studies, 15,* 381-394.

McCubbin, H. I., & McCubbin, M. A. (1988). Typologies of resilient families: Emerging roles of social class and ethnicity. *Family Relations, 37,* 247-254.

Mead, M. (1978). *Culture and commitment.* New York: Columbia University Press.

Meadows, J. L. (1991). Multicultural communication. *Physical & Occupational Therapy in Pediatrics, 11,* 31-42.

Mennen, F. E. (1988, December). The relationship of race, socioeconomic status, and marital status to kin networks. *Journal of Sociology & Social Welfare, 15,* 77-93.

Merrill, F. E. (1965). *Society and culture: An introduction to sociology* (3rd ed.). Englewood Cliffs, NJ: Prentice Hall.

Milner, D. (1983). *Children and race.* Newbury Park, CA: Sage.

Munoz, J. P., & Rios, P. (1992, August 20). Cultural diversity: In the 90's, cultural competence—Professional competence. *OT Week,* pp. 16-17.

Munroe, R. L., & Munroe, R. H. (1975). *Cross cultural human development.* Pacific Grove, CA: Brooks/Cole.

Pettitt, G. A. (1970). *Prisoners of culture.* New York: Charles Scribner.

Queen, S. A., Habenstein, R. W., & Quadagno, J. S. (1985). *The family in various cultures* (3rd ed.). New York: Harper & Row.

Ory, F. G., Simons, M., Verhulet, F. C., Leenders, F. R. H., & Woters, S. H. (1991). Children who cross cultures. *Social Science and Medicine, 32,* 29-34.

Parrillo, V. N. (1990). *Strangers to these shores: Race and ethnic relations in the USA.* New York: MacMillan.

Paulson, C. P. (1975). *Delinquency and occupational choice.* Los Angeles: University of Southern California.

Portes, P. R., Dunham, R. M., & Williams, S. (1986) Assessing child-rearing style in ecological settings: Its relation to culture, social class, early age intervention and scholastic achievement. *Adolescence, xxi,* 723-735.

Saltz, D. L. (1990, December 13). Different ethnic origins need different types of therapy. *OT Week,* p. 6.

Sanchez, V. (1964). Relevance of cultural values for occupational therapy program. *American Journal of Occupational Therapy, 18,* 1-5.

Scaff, L. A. (1989). *Fleeing the iron cage.* Los Angeles: University of California Press.

Sharff, J. W. (1981, March). Free enterprise and the ghetto family. *Psychology Today,* 41-48.

Sharma, R., & Zafar, S. (1989). A study of prejudice in relation to feelings of security-insecurity. *Journal of Personality & Clinical Studies, 5,* 73-75.

Slaugther, D. T. (1988). Programs for racially and ethnically diverse American families: Some critical issues. In I. H. B. Weiss & F. H. Jacobs, (Eds.), *Evaluating family programs* (pp. 303-314). Hawthorne, NY: Aldine.

Sparling, J. W. (1991). The cultural definition of the family. *Physical & Occupational Therapy in Pediatrics, 11,* 17-29.

Spickand, P. R. (1989). *Mixed blood: Intermarriage and ethnic identity in twentieth century America.* Madison: University of Wisconsin Press.

Stevens, G. (1985, February). Nativity, intermarriage, and mother-tongue shift. *American Sociological Review, 50,* 74-83.

Torres, R. L. R. (1989). Contributions of a bilingual COTA to an occupational therapy program. *Gerontology Special Interest Section Newsletter, 12,* 3-4.

Vandenberg, B., & Kielhofner, G. (1982). Play in evolution, culture, and individual adaptation: implications for therapy. *American Journal of Occupational Therapy, 36,* 20-28.

Vasquez, C., & Javier, R. (1991). The problem with interpreters: Communication with Spanish-speaking patients. *Hospitals and Community Psychiatry, 42,* 163-165.

Wells, S. A. (1992, September 9). The minority affairs program is just beginning. *OT Week,* p. 9.

Wells, S. A. (1992, November 19). Mentors contribute to minority practitioners' success. *OT Week,* p. 15.

Wells, S. A. (1993, January 21). Issues in minority affairs: a vision for the future. *OT Week,* p. 8.

Zinn, M. B. (1989). Family, race and poverty in the eighties. *Signs, 14,* 856-874.

Zinn, M. B., & Eitzen, D. S. (1990). *Diversity in families.* New York: Harper & Row.

X. Health Care

Anderson, J. M. (1986). Ethnicity and illness experiences: Ideological structures and the health care delivery system. *Social Science and Medicine, 22,* 1277-1283.

Axelson, J. (1985). *Counseling and development in a multicultural society.* Pacific Grove, CA: Brooks Cole.

Brown, P. A. (1976). Differential utilization of the health care delivery system by members of ethnic minorities. *Journal of Sociology and Social Welfare, 3,* 516-523.

Brownlee, A. (1978). *Community, culture and care: A cross-cultural guide for health workers.* St. Louis, MO: Mosby.

Brownlee, A. (1978b). The family and health care: Exploration in cross-cultural settings. *Social Work in Health Care, 4,* 179-198.

Campbell, S. K., & Wilhelm, I. J. (1991). Meaning of culture in pediatric rehabilitation and health care. *Physical & Occupational Therapy in Pediatrics, 11*(4), xiii.

Chavez, L. R. (1984). Undocumented immigrants and access to health services: A game of pass the buck. *Migration Today, XII,* 20-24.

Clark, A. (Ed.). (1978). *Cultural, childbearing, health professionals.* Philadelphia: F.A. Davis.

Cohen, L. M. (1979). *Culture/disease and stress among Latino immigrants.* Washington, DC: Smithsonian Institution.

Cohn, V. (1983, January). *Salvadoran health abuses reported.* The Washington Post.

Dyck, I. (1992). Managing chronic illness: An immigrant woman's acquisition and use of health care knowledge. *American Journal of Occupational Therapy, 46,* 696-705.

Devore, W., & Schilesinger, E. (1981). *Ethnic-sensitive social work practice.* St. Louis, MO: Mosby.

Egan, M. (1992, August 20). Cultural diversity: Solving medical inequities for minority groups. *OT Week,* pp. 18-19.

_____Folk medicine in the southwest: Myths and medical facts. (1985). *Postgrad-Med, 78,* 167-179.

Foster, G. (1962). *Traditional cultures and the impact of technological change.* New York: Harper & Row.

Friedman, E. (1982). Health care on the immigrant trail. *Hospitals, 56*(19), 82-84, 86-87, 90.

Gaylen, W., Glasser, I., Marcus, S., & Rothman, D. (1975). *The limits of benevolence.* New York: Harper & Row.

Giachello, A. L., Bell, R., Aday, L. A., & Andersen, R. M. (1983). Uses of the 1980 census for Hispanic health services research. *American Journal of Public Health, 73,* 266-276.

Guttmacher, S. (1983). No golden door—The health care and non-care of the undocumented. *Health/PAC Bulletin, 14*(2).

Guttmacher, S. (1984). Immigrant workers: health, law, and public policy. *International Journal of Health Services, 14,* 503-514.

Harwood, A. (Ed.). (1981). *Ethnicity and medical care.* Cambridge, MA: Harvard University Press.

Heisenberg, W. (1974). *Across the frontiers.* New York: Harper & Row.

Henderson, G. (Ed.). (1979). *Understanding and counseling ethnic minorities.* Springfield, IL: Charles C. Thomas.

Henderson, G., & Primeaux, M. (Eds.). (1981). *Transcultural health care.* Reading, MA: Addison-Wesley.

Johnson, M. (1977). Folk beliefs and ethnocultural behavior in pediatrics: Medicine or magic? *Nursing Clinics of North America, 12,* 77-84.

Kavanagh, K. H., & Kennedy, P. H. (1992). *Promoting cultural diversity: Strategies for health care professionals.* Newbury Park, CA: Sage.

Kumabe, K. T., Nishida, C., & Hepworth, D. H. (1985). *Bridging ethnocultural diversity in social work and health.* Honolulu: University of Hawaii School of Social Work.

Leininger, M. M. (Ed.). *Culture care: Diversity and universality: A theory of nursing.* New York: National League for Nursing, Pub. No. 15-2402.

Marshall, C. A., Johnson, M. J., Martin, W. E., Saravanabhavan, R. C., & Bradford, B. (1992). The rehabilitation needs of American Indians with disabilities in an urban setting. *Journal of Rehabilitation, 58*(2), 13-21.

_____Mexican folk remedies and conventional medical care. (1988). *American Family Physician, 37,* 257-262.

Morgan, S. A., & Jackson, J. (1986). Psychological and social concomitants of sickle cell anemia in adolescents. *Journal of Pediatric Psychology, 11,* 429-440.

Orque, M., Block, B., & Monrroy, L. (1983). *Ethnic nursing care: A multicultural approach.* St. Louis, MO: Mosby.

Pfefferbaum, B., Adams, J., & Aceves, J. (1990). The influence of culture on pain in Anglo and Hispanic children with cancer. *Journal of the American Academy of Child and Adolescent Psychiatry, 29,* 642-647.

Putsch, R. (1985). Cross-cultural communications. *Journal of the American Medical Association, 254,* 3344-3348.

Randall-David, E. (1989). *Strategies for working with culturally diverse communities and clients.* Washington, DC: The Association for the Care of Children's Health.

_____Rattlesnake meat ingestion—A common hispanic folk remedy. (1988). *Western Journal of Medicine, 149,* 605.

Ries, P. (1990). *Health of black and white Americans, 1985-87.* Vital and Health Statistics. Series 10, Data from the National Health Survey, 171, 114. Hyattsville, MD: U. S. Department of Health and Human Services, Public Health Service, Centers for Disease Control, National Center for Health Statistics.

Roberson, M. H. (1987). Folk health beliefs of health professionals. *Western Journal of Nursing Research, 9,* 257-263.

Scaffa, M. E., & Davis, D. A. (1990). Cultural considerations in the treatment of persons with AIDS. *Occupational Therapy in Health Care, 7,* 69-85.

Smart, J. F., & Smart, D. W. (1992, April/May/June). Cultural issues in the rehabilitation of Hispanics. *Journal of Rehabilitation, 29-37.*

Sue, D. (1981). *Counseling the culturally different: Theory and practice.* New York: Wiley.

Trevino, F. (1984). *Health indicators for hispanic, black, and white Americans.* Data from the National Health Survey, # Series 10, No. 148, DHHS Public Number PHS 84-1576. Washington, DC: U.S. Government Printing Office.

Tripp-Reimer, T. (1982). Barriers to health care: Variations in interpretation of non-Appalachian health professionals. *Western Journal of Nursing Research, 5,* 179-191.

U.S. Department of Agriculture/Department of Health & Human Services. (1986). *Cross-cultural counseling: A guide for nutrition health counselors.* Alexandria, VA: Author.

Vacc, N.A., Wittmer, J., & DeVancy, S.B. (1988). *Experiencing and counseling multicultural and diverse populations* (2nd ed.). Muncie, IN: Accelerated Development.

Wood, C. S. (1983). Early childhood, the critical state in human interactions with disease and culture. *Social Science and Medicine, 17,* 79-85.

XI. Hispanics

Acosta'Belen, E., & Sjostrom, B. (1988). *The hispanic experience in the United States: Contemporary issues and perspectives.* New York: Praeger.

Acuna, R. (1988). *Occupied America.* New York: Harper & Row.

Aguirre, B. E., & Bigelow, A. (1983). The aged in hispanic groups: A review. *International Journal of Aging and Human Development, 17,* 177-201.

Ailinger, R. L. (1989). Functional capacity of hispanic elderly immigrants. *Journal of Applied Gerontology, 8,* 97-109.

Alexander, M. A., & Black, J. J. (1988). Factors related to obesity in Mexican-American preschool children. *Image, 20,* 79-82.

Alford, H. J. (1972). *The proud peoples: The heritage and culture of spanish-speaking peoples in the United States.* New York: McKay.

Apetekar, L. (1980). How ethnic differences within a culture influence child rearing: The case of the Colombian street children. *Journal of Comparative Family Studies, 21,* 67-79.

Applewhite, S. R. (Ed.). (1988). *Hispanic elderly in transition: Theory, research, policy and practice.* Westport, CT: Greenwood.

Aquilar, I. (1972). Initial contacts with Mexican-American families. *Social Work, 17,* 66-70.

Arnold, R. R. (1983). Attitudinal research and the hispanic handicapped: A review of selected needs. *Journal of Rehabilitation, 49,* 36-38.

Bach, R. L., & Portes, A. (1985). *Latin journey: Cuban and Mexican immigrants in the United States.* Berkeley: University of California Press.

Barrera, M. (1979). *Race and class in the southwest.* Notre Dame, IN: University of Notre Dame Press.

Bastida, E. (1984). Reconstructing the social world at 60: Older Cubans in the United States. *Gerontologist, 24,* 465-470.

Bean, F.D., & Tienda, M. (1987). *The hispanic population of the United States.* New York: Russell Sage Foundation.

Bongers, L. S. (1971). *A developmental study of time perception and time perspective in three cultural groups: Anglo-American, Indian-American, Mexican-American.* Unpublished doctoral dissertation, University of California at Los Angeles.

Borjas, G., & Tienda, M. (1984). *Hispanics in the U.S. economy.* San Diego, CA: Academic Press.

Borjas, G., & Tienda, M. (1988). *Burden of support: Young Latinos in an aging society.* Stanford, CA: Stanford University Press.

Browning, R. (1984). *Protest is not enough: The struggle of blacks and hispanics for equality in the US.* Berkeley: University of California Press.

Bucklin, L. B. (1970). *Anglo and Latino: The cultural difference.* (ERIC Document Reproduction Service No. ED 044 977)

Buenning, M., & Tollefson, N. (1987). The cultural gap hypothesis as an explanation for the achievement pattern of Mexican-American students. *Psychology in the Schools, 24,* 264-272.

Burma, J. H. (Ed.). (1970). *Mexican-Americans in the United States.* Cambridge, MA: Schenkman.

Canabal, M. E. (1990). An economic approach to marital dissolution in Puerto Rico. *Journal of Marriage and the Family, 52,* 515-530.

Christensen, E. W. (1977). When counseling Puerto Ricans. *Personnel and Guidance Journal, 55,* 412-415.

Christensen, E. W. (1979). Counseling Puerto Ricans: Some cultural considerations. In G. Henderson (Ed.), *Understanding and counseling ethnic minorities* (pp. 269-279). Springfield, IL: Charles C Thomas.

Clark, M. (1979). Mexican-American family structure. In G. Henderson (Ed.), *Understanding and counseling ethnic minorities* (pp. 123-137). Springfield, IL: Charles C Thomas.

Conner, W. (Ed.). (1985). *Mexican-American in comparative perspective.* Washington, DC: Urban Institute Press.

Cortes, C. E. (Ed.). (1980). *The Cuban experience in the United States.* New York: Arno Press.

De Blassie, R. R. (1976). *Counseling with Mexican-American youth: Preconceptions and processes.* Austin, TX: Learning Concepts.

Delgado, M. (1979). Puerto Rican spiritualism and the social work profession. In G. Henderson (Ed.), *Understanding and counseling ethnic minorities* (pp. 216-231). Springfield, IL: Charles C Thomas.

Escover, P. L., & Lazarus, P. J. (1982). Cross-cultural child-rearing practices: Implications for school psychologists. *School Psychology International, 3,* 143-148.

Fitzpatrick, J. P. (1971). *Puerto Rican Americans: The meaning of migration to the mainland.* Englewood Cliffs, NJ: Prentice Hall.

Ford Foundation. (1984). *Hispanics: Challenges and opportunities.* New York: Ford Foundation Publishers.

Garcia, F. C. (1988). *Latinos and the political system.* Notre Dame, IN: Notre Dame University Press.

Goldenberg, C. N. (1987). Low-income hispanic parents' contributions to their first-grade children's word-recognition skills. *Anthropology and Education Quarterly, 18,* 149-179.

Grebler, L., More, J. W., & Guzman, R. C. (1970). *The Mexican-American people.* New York: The Free Press.

Gutierrez, J., Sameroff, A. J., & Karrer, B. M. (1988). Acculturation and SES effects on Mexican-American parents' concepts of development. *Child Development, 59,* 250-255.

Harwood, A. (1981). Mainland Puerto Ricans. In A. Harwood (Ed.), *Ethnicity and medical care* (pp. 397-481). Cambridge, MA: Harvard University Press.

Hernandez, C. A., Huang, M. J., & Wagner, N. W. (1976). *Chicanos: Social and psychological perspectives.* St. Louis, MO: Mosby.

Jaffe, A. J. (1975). *Puerto Rican population of New York City.* New York: Arno Press.

Keefe, S. E., Padilla, A. M., & Carlos, M. L. (1979). The Mexican-American extended family as an emotional support system. *Human Organization, 38,* 144-152.

Markides, K. S. (1987). Characteristics of dropouts and prediction of mortality in a longitudinal study of older Mexican Americans and Anglos. In R. A. Ward & S. Tobin (Eds.), *Health in aging: Sociological issues and policy* (pp. 86-97). New York: Springer.

Markides, K. S., Boldt, S., Joanne, S. and Ray, L. A. (1986). *Sources of helping intergenerational solidarity: A three-generations study of Mexican Americans ,41,* 506-511.

Markides, K. S., & Mindel, C. H. (1987). *Aging & ethnicity.* Newbury Park, CA: Sage.

Martinez, R. A. (1978). *Hispanic culture and health care: Fact, fiction, folklore.* St. Louis, MO: Mosby.

Massey, D. S., & Durand, J. (1987). *Return to Azatlan: The social process of international migration from western Mexico.* Berkeley: University of California Press.

Mauras-Neslen, E. (1990, December 13). An Hispanic perspective, *OT Week,* pp. 10-11.

Meyerson, M. D. (1983). Genetic counseling for families of Chicano children. In D. R. Omark & J. G. Erickson (Eds.), *The bilingual exceptional child.* San Diego, CA: College-Hill Press.

Montiel, M. (Ed.). (1978). *Hispanic families: Critical issues for policy and programs in human services.* Washington, DC: National Coalition of Hispanic Mental Health & Human Services Organizations.

Moore, J. W. (1970). *Mexican Americans.* Englewood Cliffs, NJ: Prentice Hall.

Moore, J. W., & Pachon, H. (1985). *Hispanics in the United States.* Englewood Cliffs, NJ: Prentice Hall.

O'Donnel, R. M. (1989). Functional disability among the Puerto Rican elderly. *Journal of Aging and Health, 1,* 244-264.

Padilla, A., & Keefe, S. (1987). *Chicano ethnicity.* Albuquerque, NM: University of New Mexico Press.

Padilla, F. (1985). *Latino ethnic consciousness: The case of Mexican Americans and Puerto Ricans in Chicago.* Notre Dame, IN: University of Notre Dame Press.

Padilla, F. (1987). *Puerto Rican Chicago.* Notre Dame, IN: University of Notre Dame Press.

Popka, G. W. (1980). *The evolving residential patterns of the Mexican, Puerto Rican and Cuban populations in the city of Chicago.* New York: Arno Press.

Powell, D. R., Zambrana, R., & Silva-Palacios, V. (1990). Designing culturally responsive parent programs: A comparison of low-income Mexican and Mexican-American mothers' preferences. *Family Relations, 39,* 298-304.

Rochin, R. (1988). *Economic perspective of the hispanic community.* San Antonio, TX: Tomas Rivera Center.

Rodriguez, C. (1989). *Puerto Ricans born in the USA.* Winchester, MA: Unwin and Hyman.

Rodriguez, M. (1988). Do blacks and hispanics evaluate assertive male and female characters differently? *The Howard Journal of Communications, 1,* 101-107.

Ruiz, R. (1981). Cultural and historical perspectives in counseling Hispanics. In D. Sue (Ed.), *Counseling the culturally different: Theory and practice* (pp. 186-215). New York: Wiley.

Ruiz, R. A., & Padella, A. M. (1977). Counseling Latinos. *The Personnel and Guidance Journal, 55,* 401-408.

Saenz, R. (1989). Selectivity of Mexican American intraregional migration in the southwest. *Hispanic Journal of Behavioral Sciences, 2,* 148-155.

Sanchez-Janokowski, M. (1986). *Urban bound: Political attitudes among Chicano youth.* Albuquerque, NM: University of New Mexico Press.

Sandoval, M. (1977). Afro Cuban concepts of disease and its treatment in Miami. *Journal of Operational Psychiatry, 8,* 52-63.

Sandoval, M. (1979). Santeria as a mental health care system. *Social Science and Medicine, 138,* 137-151.

Sandoval, M. (1983). Santeria. *Journal of the Florida Medical Association, 70,* 620-628.

Schreiber, J., & Homiak, J. (1981). Mexican Americans. In A. Harwood (Ed.), *Ethnicity and medical care* (pp. 264-335). Cambridge: Harvard University Press.

Seguna, D. A. (1989). Chicano and Mexican immigrant women at work: The impact of class, race, and gender on occupational mobility. *Gender and Society, 3,* 37-52.

Shapiro, J., & Tittle, K. (1990). Maternal adaptation to child disability in a hispanic population. *Family Relations, 39,* 179-185.

Silen, J. A. (1971). *We the Puerto Rican people.* New York: Monthly Review Press.

Silver, B. J., Silverman, M.M., Prescott, W., & del Pollard, L. (1985). The Cuban Immigration of 1980: A special mental health challenge. *Public Health Reports, 100,* 40-48.

Sotomayor, M., & Curiel, H. (Eds.). (1988). *Hispanic elderly: A cultural signature.* Edinburg, TX: Pan American University Press.

Staton, R. D. (1972). A comparison of Mexican and Mexican-American families. *Family Coordinator, 21,* 325-330.

Stoddard, E. (1973). *Mexican-Americans.* New York: Random House.

Teschner, R. V., Bills, G. D., & Craddock, J. R. (1975). *Spanish and English of United States Hispanos: A critical, annotated linguistic bibliography.* Arlington, VA: Center for Applied Linguistics.

Thompson-Rangel, T. (1992). The hispanic child and family: Developmental disabilities and occupational therapy intervention. *Developmental Disabilities Special Interest Section Newsletter, 15,* 2-3.

Trevino, F., Falcon, A., & Stroup-Benham (Eds.). (1990). Hispanic health and nutrition examination survey, 1982-84: Findings on health status and health care needs. *American Journal of Public Health, 80.*

Torres-Gil, F. (1986). An examination of factors affecting future cohorts of elderly hispanics. *Gerontologist, 26,* 140-146.

Trueba, H., Rodriguez, C., Zou, Y., & Cintron, J. (1993). A historical and anthropological account of a group of Mexican immigrants who managed to understand and use the United States democratic system in order to gain access to the "American dream." In *Healing multicultural America: Mexican immigrants rise to power in rural California.* Bristol, PA: Taylor & Francis.

Valle, R., & Mendoza, L. (1978). *The elder Latino.* San Diego, CA: Campanile Press.

Vega, W. A. (1990). Hispanic families in the 1980s: A decade of research. *Journal of Marriage and the Family, 52,* 1015-1024.

Wakefield, D. (1975). *Island in the city: The world of Spanish Harlem.* New York: Arno.

Wasserman, S. A. (1971). Values of Mexican-American, negro, and anglo blue-collar and white-collar children. *Child Development, 42,* 1624-1628.

Whitten, N. E. (1986). *Black frontiersmen: Afro-Hispanic culture of Ecuador and Columbia.* Prospect Heights, IL: Waveland.

XII. Managing Diversity

Jamieson, D., & O'Mara, J. (1991). How to address the needs of women, minorities, and the disabled as well as workers who differ in age, values, and education. In *Managing workforce 2000: Gaining the diversity advantage.* San Francisco: Jossey-Bass.

Loden, M., & Rosener, J. B. (1991). Emphasize diversity as an asset. In *Workforce America! Managing employee diversity as a vital resource.* Homewood, IL: Business One Irwin.

McAfee-Woods, P. (1992). A perspective of a minority in management. *Administration & Management Special Interest Section Newsletter, 8,* 2-4.

Morrison, A. (1992). *The new leaders: Guidelines on leadership diversity in America.* San Francisco: Jossey-Bass.

Thiederman, S. (1991). A practical guide to making diversity work in your company and as you deal with customers of other cultures. In *Profiting in America's multicultural marketplace: How to do business across cultural lines.* New York: Lexington.

XIII. Mental Health

Thomas, Jr., R. R. (1991). Based on work as founder and president of the American Institute for Managing Diversity. *Beyond race and gender: Unleashing the power of your total work force by managing diversity.* New York: AMACOM.

Baker, F. M. (1988). Afro-Americans. In L. Comas-Diaz & E. E. H. Griffith (Eds.), *Clinical guidelines in cross-cultural mental health* (pp. 151-181). New York: Wiley.

Baptiste, S. (1988, October). Muriel Driver memorial lecture: Chronic pain, activity and culture. *Canadian Journal of Occupational Therapy, 55,* 179-185.

Bernal, G., & Gutierrez, M. (1988). Cubans. In L. Comas-Diaz & E. E. H. Griffith (Eds.), *Clinical guidelines in cross-cultural mental health* (pp. 233-261). New York: Wiley.

Chatters, L. M. (1988). Subjective well-being evaluations among older black Americans. *Psychology and Aging, 3,* 184-190.

Dillard, M., Andonian, L., Flores, O., Lai, L., MacRae, A., & Shakir, M. (1992). Culturally competent occupational therapy in a diversely populated mental health setting. *American Journal of Occupational Therapy, 46,* 721-726.

Greene, C. L. (1935). The hand printed greeting card as a project for cases of mental and emotional deterioration in which the history indicates an intellectual and cultural background. *Occupational Therapy and Rehabilitation, 14,* 287-292.

Joe, B. E. (1992, May 7). Sensitivity alert for hispanic mental health services, *OT Week,* p. 10.

Katz, N., Giladi, N., & Peretz, C. (1988). Cross-cultural application of occupational therapy assessments: Human occupation with psychiatric inpatients and controls in Israel. *Occupational Therapy in Mental Health, 8,* 7-30.

Martinez, C. (1988). Mexican-Americans. In L. Comas-Diaz & E. E. H. Griffith (Eds.), *Clinical guidelines in cross-cultural mental health* (pp. 182-203). New York: Wiley.

Mollica, R. F., & Lavelle, J. (1988). Southeast Asian refugees. In L. Comas-Diaz & E. E. H. Griffith (Eds.), *Clinical guidelines in cross-cultural mental health* (pp. 262-293). New York: Wiley.

Niemeyer, L. O. (1990). Psychologic and sociocultural aspects of responses to pain. *Occupational Therapy Practice, 1*(3), 11-20.

Ramos-McKay, J. M., Comas-Diaz, L., & Rivera, L. A. (1988). Puerto Ricans. In L. Comas-Diaz & E. E. H. Griffith (Eds.), *Clinical guidelines in cross-cultural mental health* (pp. 205-232). New York: Wiley.

Rhoades, E. R. (1980). Mental health problems of American Indians seen in outpatient facilities of the Indian Health Service, 1975. *Public Health Reports, 95,* 329-335.

Rhoades, E. R., Marshall, M., Attneave, C., Echohawk, N., & Bjork, J. (1980). Impact of mental disorders upon elderly American Indians as reflected in visits to ambulatory care facilities. *American Geriatrics Society Journal, 28,* 33-39.

Roger, L. H., Cortes, D. E., & Malgady, R. G. (1991). Acculturation and mental health status among hispanics. *American Psychologist, 46*(6), 585-591.

Rosenstein, M. J. (1980). Hispanic Americans and mental health services: A comparison of hispanic, black, and white admissions to selected mental health facilities, 1975. *Series CN: Mental Health Statistics No. 3,* iv; 45. Rockville, MD: U.S. Department of Health and Human Services.

Seccombe, K. (1989). Ethnicity or socioeconomic status? Health differentials between elder Alaska natives and whites. *Gerontologist, 29,* 551-556.

Serafica, F. C., Schwebel, A. I., Russell, R. K., Isaac, P. D., & Myers, L. B. (1990). *Mental health of ethnic minorities.* New York: Praeger.

Shih, L. S. (1984). Mood and affect following success and failure in two cultural groups. *Occupational Therapy Journal of Research, 4,* 213-230.

Steinberg, A. (1991). Issues in providing mental services to hearing-impaired persons. *Hospital and Community Psychiatry, 42,* 380-389.

Stiffman, A. R., & Davis, L. E. (1990). *Ethnic issues in adolescent mental health.* Newbury Park, CA: Sage.

Strong, C. (1984). Stress and caring for elderly relatives: Interpretations and coping strategies in an American Indian and white sample. *Gerontologist, 24,* 251-256.

Vargas, G. E. (1984). Recently arrived Central American immigrants: Mental health needs. *Research Bulletin,* Spanish Speaking Mental Health Research Center.

Yee, B. W. K., & Hennessey, S. T. (1982). Pacific/Asian American families and mental health. In F. U. Munoz & R. Endo (Eds.), *Perspectives on minority group mental health* (pp. 53-70). Washington, DC: University Press of America.

XIV. Native Americans

Bachtold, L. M. (1984). Antecedents of caregiver attitudes and social behavior of Hupa Indian and Anglo-American preschoolers in California. *Child Study Journal, 13,* 217-233.

Bongers, L. S. (1971). *A developmental study of time perception and time perspective in three cultural groups: Anglo-American, Indian-American, Mexican-American.* Unpublished doctoral dissertation, University of California at Los Angeles.

Brown, D. (1970). *Bury my heart at Wounded Knee.* Fort Worth, TX: Holt, Rinehart & Winston.

Bureau of Indian Affairs. (1978). *Information about Indians.* Washington, DC: Author.

Courlander, H. (1982). *Hopi voices: Recollections, traditions and narratives of the Hopi Indians.* Albuquerque, NM: University of New Mexico Press.

Deloria, V. (1979). *The metaphysics of modern existence.* New York: Harper & Row.

Deloria, V., & Lytle, C. (1984). *The nation within: The past and future of American Indian sovereignty.* New York: Pantheon.

Dorris, M. (1989). *The broken cord.* New York: Harper & Row.

Dozier, E. P. (1970). *The Pueblo Indians of North America.* New York: Holt, Rinehart & Winston.

Dukepoo, F. (1978). *The elder American Indian.* San Diego, CA: Campanile.

Dukepoo, F. (1980). *The elderly American Indian.* San Diego, CA: San Diego State University, University Center on Aging.

Dumont, R. V. (1972). Learning English and how to be silent: Studies in Sioux and Cherokee classrooms. In C. B. Cazden, V. P. John, & D. Hymes (Eds.), *Functions of language in the classroom.* New York: Columbia Teachers College.

Dutton, B. P. (1975). *Indians of the American Southwest.* Englewood Cliffs, NJ: Prentice Hall.

Edwards, E. E., Edwards, M. E., & Daines, G. M. (1980). American Indian/Alaska native elderly: A current and vital concern. *Journal of Gerontological Social Work, 2,* 213-224.

Gill, S. D. (1983). *Native American traditions: Source and interpretations.* Belmont, CA: Wadsworth.

Gupta, O. K., & Gupta, S. O. (1985). A study of the influence of American culture on the child-rearing attitudes of Indian mothers. *Indian Journal of Social Work, 46,* 95-104.

Harris, G. A. (1986). The aging minority: American Indian perspective/community-based rehabilitation solution. Concerns for minority groups in communication disorders. *ASHA Reports, 16,* 22-26.

Havighurst, R. J. (1974). The American Indian: From assimilation to cultural pluralism. *Educational Leadership, 31,* 585-589.

Heard, J. N. (1987). *Handbook of the American frontier—Four centuries of Indian-white relationships: The southeastern woodlands.* Metuchen, NJ: Scarecrow.

Heckewelder, J. G. E. (1971). *History, manners, and customs of the Indian nations who once inhabited Pennsylvania and the neighboring states.* New York: Arno.

Hogan, W. T. (1979). *American Indians.* Chicago: University of Chicago Press.

Hudson, C. M. (1976). *The southeastern Indians.* Knoxville, TN: University of Tennessee Press.

Huttling, K., Krefting, L., Drevdahl, D., Tree, P., Baca, E., & Benally, E. (1992). "Doing battle": A metaphorical analysis of diabetes mellitus among Navajo people. *American Journal of Occupational Therapy, 46,* 706-712.

Irvine, K. (1974). *Encyclopedia of the Indians of the Americas.* St. Clair Shores, MI: Scholarly Press.

Johnson, F. L., Cook, E., Foxall, M. J., Kelleher, E., & Kentopp, E. (1986). Life satisfaction of the elderly American Indian. *International Journal of Nursing Studies, 23,* 265-273.

Jorgensen, J. G. (1980). Western Indians: *Comparative environments, languages and cultures of 172 western American Indian tribes.* San Francisco, CA: W. H. Freeman.

Josephy, A. M., Jr. (1982). *Now that the buffalo's gone: A study of today's American Indians.* New York: Alfred A. Knopf.

Kamo, Y., Borgatta, E. F., Montgomery, R. J. V., & Seccombe, K. (1988). Profile of Alaska's seniors: 2. Housing, and its correlates. *Research on Aging, 10,* 517-533.

Kramer, J. M. (1988). Infant mortality and risk factors among American Indians compared to black and white rates; implications for policy change. In W. A. Van Horne & Y. V. Tonnesen (Eds.), *Ethnicity and health* (pp. 89-115). Madison, WI: University of Wisconsin System Institute on Race and Ethnicity.

Krauss, M. E., & McGary, M. J. (1980). *Alaska native languages: A bibliographical catalogue.* Fairbanks, AK: Alaska Native Language Center.

Kunitz, S., & Levy, J. (1981). Navajos. In A. Harwood (Ed.), *Ethnicity and medical care* (pp. 337-397). Cambridge, MA: Harvard University Press.

Lamarine, R. J. (1987). Self-esteem, health locus of control, and health attitudes among Native American children. *Journal of School Health, 57,* 371-374.

Linton, M. (1970). *Problems of Indian children.* (ERIC Document Reproduction Service No. ED 044 727).

Manson, S. M. (1989). Long-term care in American Indian communities: Issues for planning and research. *Gerontologist, 29,* 38-44.

Matthiessen, P. (1984). *Indian country.* New York: Viking.

McNeil, W. H. (1976). *Plagues and peoples.* New York: Doubleday.

McNickle, D. (1973). *Native American tribalism: Indian survivals and renewals.* London: Oxford University Press.

Miller, D. (1975). Native American families in the city. In G. Powell, J. Yamamoto, A. Romero, & A. Morales (Eds.), *The psychological development of minority group children.* New York: Brunner/Mazel.

Miller, M. R. (1970). The language and language beliefs of Indian children. *Anthropological Linguistics, 12,* 51-61.

Mitra, S. K. (1985). Indian personality: A perspective. *Samiska, 39,* 31-55.

Montgomery, R. J. V., Borgatta, E. F., Yamo, Y., & Seccombe, K. (1988). Profile of Alaska's seniors: 3. Income, children and health. *Research on Aging, 10,* 534-549.

Montgomery, R. J. V., Seccombe, K., Borgatta, E. F., & Yamo, Y. (1988). Profile of Alaska's seniors. *Research on Aging, 10,* 275-296.

Nabokov, P. (1979). *Native American testimony—An anthology of Indian and White relations: First encounter to dispossession.* New York: Harper & Row.

National Indian Council on Aging. (1981). *American Indian elderly: A national profile.* Albuquerque, NM: Author.

National Lawyers Guild, Committee on Native American Struggles. (Ed.). (1982). *Rethinking Indian law.* New Haven, CT: Advocate Press.

Nelson, R. K. (1980). *Shadow of the hunter: stories of Eskimo life.* Chicago: University of Chicago Press.

Nichols, D. A. (1978). *Lincoln and the Indians: Civil war policy and politics.* Columbia, MO: University of Missouri Press.

Nystul, M. S. (1982). Ten Adlerian parent-child principles applied to Navajos. *Individual Psychology Journal of Adlerian Theory, Research and Practice, 38,* 183-189.

Primeaux, M. (1977a). American Indian health care practices: A cross-cultural perspective. *Nursing Clinics of North America, 12,* 55-65.

Primeaux, M. (1977b). Caring for the American Indian patient. *American Journal of Nursing, 77,* 91-96.

Porter, F. (1983). *Maryland Indians: Yesterday and today.* Baltimore, MD: Museum and Library of Maryland History, The Maryland Historical Society.

Red Horse, J. G. (1978). Family behavior of urban American Indians. *Social Casework, 59,* 67-72.

Red Horse, J. G. (1980). American Indian elders: Unifiers of Indian families. *Social Casework, 61,* 490-493.

Red Horse, J., Lewis, R., Feit, M., & Decker, J. (1978). Family behavior of urban American Indians. *Social Casework, 59,* 67-72.

Richardson, E. (1981). Cultural and historical perspectives in counseling American Indians. In D. Sue (Ed.), *Counseling the culturally different* (pp. 216-255). New York: Wiley.

Savage, W. W., Jr. (1977). *Indian life: Transforming an American myth.* Norman, OK: University of Oklahoma.

Spencer, R. F. (1977). *The Native American: Ethnology and backgrounds of North American Indians.* New York: Harper & Row.

Thompson, T. (1978). *The schooling of native America.* Washington, DC: American Association of Colleges for Teachers of English in collaboration with The Teacher Corps., U.S. Office of Education.

Thornton, R. (1987). *American Indian holocaust and survival: A population history since 1492.* Norman, OK: Oklahoma Press.

Trimble, J. (1976). Value differentials and their importance in counseling American Indians. In P. Pederson, J. Draguns, W. Lonner, & J. Trimble (Eds.), *Counseling across cultures* (pp. 201-226). Honolulu: University of Hawaii Press.

Waddell, J. O., & Watson, O. M. (1971). *The American Indian in urban society.* Boston: Little, Brown.

Wax, M. L. (1971). *Indian Americans: Unity and diversity.* Englewood Cliffs, NJ: Prentice-Hall.

Weatherford, J. (1988). *Indian givers: How Indians of the Americas transformed the world.* New York: Crown.

Weaver, T. (Ed.). (1974). *Indians of Arizona: A contemporary perspective.* Tucson: University of Arizona Press.

Woodcock, G. (1977). *Peoples of the coast: The Indians of the pacific Northwest.* Bloomington, IN: Indiana University Press.

Youngman, G., & Sadonge, M. (1974). Counseling the American Indian child. *Elementary School Guidance and Counseling, 9,* 272.

XV. Other

Armstrong, P., & Feldman, S. (1986). *A midwife's story.* New York: Arbor House.

Baptiste, D. (1987). Pyschotherapy with gay/lesbian couples and their children in step-families: A challenge for marriage and family therapists. *Journal of Homosexuality, 146,* 223-238.

Caldwell, M., & Peplau, L. (1984). The balance of power in lesbian relationships. *Sex Roles, 10,* 587-599.

Candell, M., Finn, S., & Marecek, J. (1981). Sex-role identity, sex-role behavior, and satisfaction in heterosexual, lesbian and gay male couples. *Psychology of Women Quarterly, 5,* 488-491.

Hare, J., & Koepke, L. (1990). Susanne and her two mothers. *Day Care and Early Education, 18,* 20-21.

Hostetler, J. (1980). *Amish society. Baltimore:* Johns Hopkins University Press.

Huntington, G. (1976). The Amish family. In C. H. Mendel & R. W. Haberstein (Eds.), *Ethnic families in America.* New York: Elsevier.

Jungersen, K. (1992). Culture, theory, and the practice of occupational therapy in New Zealand/Aotearoa. *American Journal of Occupational Therapy, 46,* 745-750.

Kelly, J. (1972). Sisterlove: An exploration of the need for homosexual experience. *Family Coordinator, 21,* 472-475.

Koepke, L., Hare, J., & Moran, P. B. (1992). Relationship quality in a sample of lesbian couples with children and child-free lesbian couples. *Family Relations, 41,* 224-229.

Moses, A., & Hawkins, R. (1982). *Counseling lesbian women and gay men: A life-issue approach.* Columbus, OH: Charles E. Merrill

Rogers, C. J., Barstow, S. L., & Gross, G. E. (1992, January 16). Cultural diversity: Health care in Amish country. *OT Week,* pp. 24-25.

Smith, E. (1960). *Studies in Amish demography.* Harrisonburg, VA: Research Council, East Mennonite College.

Warner, J., & Denlinger, D. (1969). *The gentle people: A portrait of the Amish.* New York: Grossman.

Wittmer, J. (1970). Homogeneity of personality characteristics: A comparison between old order Amish and non-Amish. *American Anthropologist, 72,* 1063-1067.

Yelton, D., & Nielson, C. (1991). Understanding Appalachian values—Implications for occupational therapists. *Occupational Therapy in Mental Health, 11,* 173-195.

XVI. Racial/ Ethnic Impact

Asante, M. K., (Ed.). (1979). *Handbook of intercultural communication.* Beverly Hills, CA: Sage.

Brown, P. A. (1976). Differential utilization of the health care delivery system by members of ethnic minorities. *Journal of Sociology and Social Welfare, 3,* 516-523.

Brownlee, A. (1978a). *Community, culture and care: A cross-cultural guide for health workers.* St. Louis, MO: Mosby.

Brownlee, A. (1978b). The family and health care: Exploration in cross-cultural settings. *Social Work in Health Care, 4,* 179-198.

Clark, A. (Ed.). (1978). *Culture, childbearing, health professionals.* Philadelphia: F.A. Davis.

Daedalus Editorial Board. (1981). American Indians, blacks, Chicanos, and Puerto Ricans [Special issue]. *Daedalus, 110*(2).

Dana, R. H. (1981). *Human services for cultural minorities.* Baltimore: University Park Press.

Dunbar, L. W. (Ed.). (1984). *Minority report: What's happened to Blacks, Hispanics, American Indians, and other American minorities.* New York: Pantheon Books.

Dworkin, A. G., & Dworkin, R. J. (1982). *Minority report: An introduction to racial, ethnic, & gender relations* (2nd ed.). Fort Worth, TX: Holt, Rinehart & Winston.

Farley, R., & Allen, W. R. (1987). *The color line and the quality of life in America.* New York: Russell Sage Foundation.

Feagin, J. R. (1984). *Racial and ethnic relations.* Englewood Cliffs, NJ: Prentice Hall.

Foner, N. (Ed.). (1984). *New immigrants in New York.* New York: Columbia University Press.

Gelfand, D. E. (1982). *Aging: The ethnic factor.* Boston, MA: Little Brown.

Gonzales, G. (1974). Language, culture, and exceptional children. *Exceptional Children, 40,* 565.

Grasska, M., & McFarland, T. (1982). Overcoming the language barrier: Problems and solutions. *American Journal of Nursing, 82,* 1376-1379.

Gray, E., & Cosgrove, J. (1985). Ethnocentric perception of childrearing practices in protective services. *Child Abuse and Neglect, 9,* 389-396.

Hall, W., & Nagy, W. (1981). Cultural differences in communication. *New York University Education Quarterly, 13,* 16-22.

Harwood, A. (Ed.). (1981). *Ethnicity and medical care.* Cambridge, MA: Harvard University Press.

Henderson, G. (Ed.). (1979). *Understanding and counseling ethnic minorities.* Springfield, IL: Charles C Thomas.

Henderson, G., & Primeaux, M. (Eds.). (1981). *Transcultural health care.* Reading, MA: Addison-Wesley.

Janosik, E. H. (1980). Variations in ethnic families. In J.R. Miller & E. H. Janosik (Eds.), *Family focused care* (pp. 58-101). New York: McGraw-Hill.

Jenkins, S., & Morrison, B. (1978). Ethnicity and service delivery. *American Journal of Orthopsychiatry, 48,* 160-165.

Kessner, T., & Caroli, B. B. (1981) *Today's immigrants, their stories: A new look at the newest Americans.* New York: Oxford University Press.

Kleinman, A., Eisenberg, L., & Good, G. (1978). Culture, illness and care: Clinical lessons from anthropologic and cross-cultural research. *Annals of Internal Medicine, 88,* 251-258.

Kohls, L. R. (1981). *Developing intercultural awareness.* Washington, DC: Society for Intercultural Education, Training and Research.

Kohls, L. R. (1984). *The values Americans live by.* Washington, DC: Meridian House International.

Kumabe, K. T., Nishida, C., & Hepworth, D. H. (1985). *Bridging ethnocultural diversity in social work and health.* Honolulu: University of Hawaii School of Social Work.

Kuper, J. (1985). *Race and race relations.* London: Batsford Academic and Education.

Laguerre, M. (1981). Haitian Americans. In A. Harwood (Ed.), *Ethnicity and medical care* (pp. 172-210). Cambridge, MA: Harvard University Press.

Lieberson, S. (1980). *A piece of the pie: Blacks and white immigrants since 1980.* Berkeley: University of California Press.

Lieberson, S., & Waters, M. (1988). *From many strands: Ethnic and racial groups in contemporary America.* New York: Russell Sage Foundation.

Mendel, C. H., & Haberstein, R. W. (1976). *Ethnic families in America.* New York: Elsevier.

Myerhoff, B. (1978). Aging and the aged in other cultures: An anthropological perspective. In E. E. Bauwens (Ed.), *The anthropology of health.* St. Louis, MO: Mosby.

Orque, M., Block. B., & Monrroy, L. (1983). *Ethnic nursing care: A multicultural approach.* St. Louis, MO: Mosby.

Pederson, P., Draguns, J., Lonner, W., & Trimble, J. (1976). *Counseling across cultures.* Honolulu, HI: University of Hawaii Press.

Porteus, S. D. (1984). *Ethnic group differences.* Brooklyn, NY: Revisionist Press.

Putsch, R. (1985). Cross-cultural communications. *Journal of the American Medical Association, 254,* 3344-3348.

Quesada, G. M. (1976). Language and communication barriers for health delivery to a minority group. *Social Science and Medicine, 10,* 323-327.

Roberson, M. H. (1987). Folk health beliefs of health professionals. *Western Journal of Nursing Research, 9,* 257-263.

Robinson, G. L. N. (1985). *Crosscultural understanding.* New York: Pergammon.

Schuman, H., Steen, C., & Bobo, L. (1985). *Racial attitudes in America: Trends and interpretations.* Cambridge, MA: Harvard University Press.

Schusky, E.L., & Culbert, T. P. (1978). *Introducing culture.* Englewood Cliffs, NJ: Prentice Hall.

Scott, C. (1974). Health and healing practices among five ethnic groups in Miami, Florida. *Public Health Reports, 89,* 524-532.

Simpson, G. E., & Yinger M. J. (1985). *Racial and cultural minorities: An analysis of prejudice and discrimination.* New York: Plenum.

Sollors, W. (1986). *Beyond ethnicity: consent and descent in American culture.* New York: Oxford University Press.

Sowell, T. (1981). *Ethnic America: A history.* New York: Basic Books.

Spector, R. E. (1985). *Cultural diversity in health and illness* (2nd ed.). Norwalk, CT: Appleton-Century-Crofts.

Stewart, E. C. (1972). *American cultural patterns—A cross-cultural perspective.* Yarmouth, ME: Intercultural Press.

Steinberg, S. (1981). *The ethnic myth: Race, ethnicity and class in America.* Boston: Beacon.

Sue, D. (1981). *Counseling the culturally different: Theory and practice.* New York: Wiley.

Taylor, R. B. (1976). *Cultural ways: A concise edition of introduction to cultural anthropology.* Boston: Allyn & Bacon.

U.S. Department of Agriculture, & Department of Health and Human Services. (1986). *Cross-cultural counseling: A guide for nutrition and health counselors.* Washington, DC: Author.

Watkins, E. L., & Johnson, A. E. (Eds.). (1979). *Removing cultural and ethnic barriers to health care.* Proceedings of a National Conference. Chapel Hill, NC: University of North Carolina.

XVII. Workforce

Bullock, P. (1973). Aspiration vs. opportunity: "Careers" in the inner city. *Policy papers in human resources and industrial relations, 20,* 173. Ann Arbor, MI: Institute of Labor and Industrial Relations, The University of Michigan-Wayne State University.

Cultural diversity at work. (Aimed at preparing readers for managing, training and conducting business in the global age.) Newsletter, 13751 Lake City Way NE, Suite 106, Seattle, WA 98125-3615.

David, G., & Watson, G. (1982). *Black life in corporate America.* Garden City, NY: Doubleday, Anchor Press.

Fernandez, J. (1981). *Racism and sexism in corporate life.* Lexington, MA: Lexington Books.

Fraser, I. (1943). Employment of the disabled. *Occupational Therapy and Rehabilitation, 22,* 280-285.

Hardesty, S., & Jacobs, N. (1986). *Success and betrayal: The crisis of women in corporate America.* New York: Franklin Watts.

Harris, P. R., & Moran, R. T. (1987). *Managing cultural differences.* Houston, TX: Gulf Publishing.

Johnston, W. B., & Packer, A. E. (1987). *Workforce 2000: Work and workers for the twenty-first century.* Indianapolis, IN: Hudson Institute.

Kanter, R. M. (1977). *Men and women of the corporation.* New York: Basic Books.

Katz, J. H. (1978). *White awareness: A handbook for anti-racism.* Norman, OK: University of Oklahoma Press.

Loden, M. (1985). *Feminine leadership or how to succeed in business without being one of the boys.* New York: Times Books.

Loden, M., & Rosener, J. (1991). *Workforce America: Managing employee diversity as a vital resource.* Homewood, IL.

Managing diversity. Managing diverse work forces. Newsletter. P.O. Box 819, Jamestown, NY 14702-0819; 1-800-542-7869.

Utley, E. R. (1974). *A comparison of the values held by black employees and white management in five state hospitals in Ohio.* Columbus, OH: Ohio State University.

Wallace, P. A. (1980). *Black women in the labor force.* Cambridge, MA: MIT Press.

XVIII. Videotapes

Barr Films. *Bridging cultural barriers: Managing ethnic diversity in the workplace.* 1280 Schabarm Avenue, Irwindale, CA. 91706-7878.

Griggs Productions. *Valuing diversity* (Film). 302 23rd Ave., San Francisco, CA 94121; (415) 668-4200.

Black Issues in Higher Education. 10520 Warwick Ave., Suite B-8, Fairfax, VA 22030; (703) 385-2981:

Enhancing Race Relations on Campus.

Men of Color: Absence in Academia.

The Rise in Campus Racism: Causes & Solutions.

The State of Black Health Care.

Recruiting & Retaining Minority Students, Faculty & Administrators: Strategies for the 90's.